DUDLEY PUBLIC LIBRARIES

The loan of this book may be renewed if not required by other readers, by contacting the library from which it was borrowed.

D0767559

000000740547

hamlyn | **all colour cookbook**

200 Light
healthy curries

An Hachette UK Company
www.hachette.co.uk

First published in Great Britain in 2015 by Hamlyn
a division of Octopus Publishing Group Ltd
Endeavour House, 189 Shaftesbury Avenue
London WC2H 8JY
www.octopusbooks.co.uk

Copyright © Octopus Publishing Group Ltd 2015

Recipes in this book have previously appeared in other
books by Hamlyn.

ISBN: 978-0-600-62896-5

A CIP catalogue record for this book is available from the
British Library.

Printed and bound in China.

10 9 8 7 6 5 4 3 2 1

Both metric and imperial measurements have been given
in all recipes. Use one set of measurements only, and not a
mixture of both.

Standard level spoon measurements are used in all recipes
1 tablespoon = 15 ml spoon
1 teaspoon = 5 ml spoon

Ovens should be preheated to the specified temperature
– if using a fan-assisted oven, follow the manufacturer's
instructions for adjusting the time and temperature.

Fresh herbs, medium eggs and freshly ground black pepper
should be used unless otherwise stated.

This book includes dishes made with nuts and nut
derivatives. It is advisable for people with known allergic
reactions to nuts and nut derivatives or those who may be
potentially vulnerable to these allergies, such as pregnant
and nursing mothers, invalids, the elderly, babies and
children, to avoid dishes made with these. It is prudent
to check the labels of all pre-prepared ingredients for the
possible inclusion of nut derivatives.

contents

introduction

introduction

this series

The Hamlyn All Colour Light Series is a collection of handy-sized books, each packed with over 200 healthy recipes on a variety of topics and cuisines to suit your needs.

The books are designed to help those people who are trying to lose weight by offering a range of delicious recipes that are low in calories but still high in flavour. The recipes show a calorie count per portion, so you will know exactly what you are eating. These are recipes for real and delicious food, not ultra-slimming meals, so they will help you maintain your new healthier eating plan for life. They must be used as part of a balanced diet, with the cakes and sweet dishes eaten only as an occasional treat.

how to use this book

All the recipes in this book are clearly marked with the number of calories (kcal) per serving. The chapters cover different calorie bands: Under 500 calories, under 400 calories, etc.

Many recipes have variations at the bottom of the page – note the calorie count as they do vary and can sometimes be more than the original recipe.

The figures assume that you are using low-fat versions of dairy products, so be sure to use skimmed milk and low-fat yogurt. They have also been calculated using lean meat, so make sure you trim meat of all visible fat

and remove the skin from chicken breasts. Use moderate amounts of oil and butter for cooking and low-fat/low-calorie alternatives when you can.

Don't forget to take note of the number of portions each recipe makes and divide up the quantity of food accordingly, so that you know just how many calories you are consuming.

Be careful about side dishes and accompaniments that will also add to the calorie content.

Above all, enjoy trying out the new flavours and exciting recipes that this book contains. Rather than dwelling on the thought that you are denying yourself your usual unhealthy treats, think of your new regime as a positive step towards a new you. Not only will you lose weight and feel more confident, but your health will benefit, the condition of your hair and nails will improve, and you will take on a healthy glow.

the risks of obesity

Up to half of all women and two-thirds of men are overweight or obese in the developed world today. Being overweight can not only make us unhappy with our appearance, but can also lead to serious health problems, including heart disease, high blood pressure and diabetes.

When someone is obese, it means they are overweight to the point that it could start to seriously threaten their health. In fact, obesity ranks as a close second to smoking as a possible cause of cancer. Obese women are more likely to have complications during and after pregnancy, and people who are overweight or obese are also more likely to suffer from coronary heart disease, gallstones, osteoarthritis, high blood pressure and type 2 diabetes.

how can I tell if I am overweight?

The best way to tell if you are overweight is to work out your body mass index (BMI). If using metric measurements, divide your weight in kilograms (kg) by your height in metres (m) squared. (For example, if you are 1.7 m tall and weigh 70 kg, the calculation would be 70 ÷ 2.89 = 24.2.) If using imperial measurements, divide your weight in pounds (lb) by your height in inches (in) squared and multiply by 703. Then compare the figure to the list below (these figures apply to healthy adults only).

Less than 20	underweight
20–25	healthy
25–30	overweight
Over 30	obese

As we all know by now, one of the major causes of obesity is eating too many calories.

what is a calorie?

Our bodies need energy to stay alive, grow, keep warm and be active. We get the energy we need to survive from the food and drinks we consume – more specifically, from the fat, carbohydrate, protein and alcohol that they contain.

A calorie (cal), as anyone who has ever been on a diet will know, is the unit used to measure how much energy different foods contain. A calorie can be scientifically defined as the energy required to raise the temperature of 1 gram of water from 14.5°C to 15.5°C. A kilocalorie (kcal) is 1,000 calories and it is, in fact, kilocalories that we usually mean when we talk about the calories in different foods.

Different food types contain different numbers of calories. For example, a gram of carbohydrate (starch or sugar) provides 3.75 kcal, protein provides 4 kcal per gram, fat provides 9 kcal per gram and alcohol provides 7 kcal per gram. So, fat is the most concentrated source of energy – weight for weight, it provides just over twice as many calories as either protein or carbohydrate –

with alcohol not far behind. The energy content of a food or drink depends on how many grams of carbohydrate, fat, protein and alcohol are present.

how many calories do we need?

The number of calories we need to consume varies from person to person, but your body weight is a clear indication of whether you are eating the right amount. Body weight is simply determined by the number of calories you are eating compared to the number of calories your body is using to maintain itself and needed for physical activity. If you regularly consume more calories than you use up, you will start to gain weight as extra energy is stored in the body as fat.

Based on our relatively inactive modern-day lifestyles, most nutritionists recommend that women should aim to consume around 2,000 calories (kcal) per day, and men an amount of around 2,500. Of course, the amount of energy required depends on your level of activity: the more active you are, the more energy you need to maintain a stable weight.

a healthier lifestyle

To maintain a healthy body weight, we need to expend as much energy as we eat; to lose weight, energy expenditure must therefore exceed intake of calories. So, exercise is a vital tool in the fight to lose weight. Physical activity doesn't just help us control body weight; it also helps to reduce our appetite and is known to have beneficial effects on the heart and blood that help prevent against cardiovascular disease.

Many of us claim we don't enjoy exercise and simply don't have the time to fit it into our hectic schedules. So the easiest way to increase physical activity is by incorporating it into our daily routines, perhaps by walking or cycling instead of driving (particularly for short journeys), taking up more active hobbies such as gardening, and taking small and simple steps, such as using the stairs instead of the lift whenever possible.

As a general guide, adults should aim to undertake at least 30 minutes of moderate-intensity exercise, such as a brisk walk, five times a week. The 30 minutes does not have to be taken all at once: three sessions of 10 minutes are equally beneficial. Children and young people should be encouraged to

take at least 60 minutes of moderate-intensity exercise every day.

Some activities will use up more energy than others. The following list shows some examples of the energy a person weighing 60 kg (132 lb) would expend doing the following activities for 30 minutes:

activity	energy
ironing	69 kcal
cleaning	75 kcal
walking	99 kcal
golf	129 kcal
fast walking	150 kcal
cycling	180 kcal
aerobics	195 kcal
swimming	195 kcal
running	300 kcal
sprinting	405 kcal

make changes for life

The best way to lose weight is to try to adopt healthier eating habits that you can easily maintain all the time, not just when you are trying to slim down. Aim to lose no more than 1 kg (2 lb) per week to ensure you lose only your fat stores. People who go on crash diets lose lean muscle as well as fat and are much more likely to put the weight back on again soon afterwards.

For a woman, the aim is to reduce her daily calorie intake to around 1,500 kcal while she is trying to lose weight, then settle on around 2,000 per day thereafter to maintain her new body weight. Regular exercise will also make a huge difference: the more you can burn, the less you will need to diet.

improve your diet

For most of us, simply adopting a more balanced diet will reduce our calorie intake and lead to weight loss. Follow these simple recommendations:

Eat more starchy foods, such as bread, potatoes, rice and pasta. Assuming these replace the fattier foods you usually eat, and you don't smother them with oil or butter, this will help reduce the amount of fat and increase the amount of fibre in your diet. As a bonus, try to use wholegrain rice, pasta and flour, as the energy from these foods is released more slowly in the body, making you feel fuller for longer.

11

Eat more fruit and vegetables, aiming for at least five portions of different fruit and vegetables a day (excluding potatoes).

As long as you don't add extra fat to your fruit and vegetables in the form of cream, butter or oil, these changes will help reduce your fat intake and increase the amount of fibre and vitamins you consume.

who said vegetables must be dull?

Eat fewer sugary foods, such as biscuits, cakes and chocolate bars. This will also help reduce your fat intake. If you fancy something sweet, choose fresh or dried fruit instead.

Reduce the amount of fat in your diet, so you consume fewer calories. Low-fat versions are available for most dairy products, including milk, cheese, crème fraîche, yogurt, and even cream and butter. Choose these in favour of full-fat versions; it doesn't necessarily mean your food will be tasteless.

Choose lean cuts of meat, such as back bacon instead of streaky, and chicken breasts instead of thighs. Trim all visible fat off meat before cooking and avoid frying foods – grill or roast instead. Fish is also naturally low in fat and can make a variety of tempting dishes.

simple steps to reduce your intake

Few of us have an iron will, so when you are trying to cut down make it easier on yourself by following these steps:

- Serve small portions to start with. You may feel satisfied when you have finished, but if you are still hungry you can always go back for more.
- Once you have served up your meal, put away any leftover food before you eat. Don't put heaped serving dishes on the table, as you will undoubtedly pick, even if you feel satisfied with what you have already eaten.
- Eat slowly and savour your food; then you are more likely to feel full when you have finished. If you rush a meal, you may still feel hungry afterwards.
- Make an effort with your meals. Just because you are cutting down doesn't mean your meals have to be low on taste as well as calories. You will feel more satisfied with a meal you have really enjoyed and will be less likely to look for comfort in a bag of crisps or a bar of chocolate.
- Plan your meals in advance to make sure you have all the ingredients you need. Casting around in the cupboards when you are hungry is unlikely to result in a healthy, balanced meal.
- Keep healthy and interesting snacks to hand for those moments when you need something to pep you up. You don't need to succumb to a chocolate bar if there are other tempting treats on offer.

curries

Originating from the South Indian Tamil word *kari*, which means gravy or sauce, the word 'curry' literally refers to the spice blend used to flavour a dish. The word has evolved to describe a wide variety of saucy, spiced dishes from all over India, Southeast Asia, and even as far as Japan. We once used the word to describe an entire cuisine, but recently we have begun to discover the true diversity of our favourite food, and we are being introduced to authentic recipes from the many countries that provide spicy dishes that fall under the 'curry' umbrella.

A common perception is that a curry is a hot and spicy dish. Yes, you can eat a curry that will blow your socks off but, on the whole, most curry recipes are delicate and highly sophisticated, containing a balanced blend of spices and herbs.

As food lovers today, we have embraced curries from all over the world and count them among our favourite foods. There is nothing more satisfying to me than producing a rich, aromatic curry to share with friends and family.

Whatever its origins, a curry usually has a selection of fresh and dried herbs and spices. Depending on the dish, other ingredients could include chillies, curry leaves, ginger, garlic, shallots, lemon grass, coconut milk, palm sugar, tamarind paste, Thai fish sauce, shrimp paste and chopped tomatoes. The recipes and ingredients vary from region to region, as well as from country to country.

As knowledgeable and passionate food lovers today, we have embraced curries from all over the world. You can buy most of the ingredients in any large supermarket, and with the miracle of Internet shopping you can even order exotic ingredients and have them delivered to your door.

This book offers exciting recipes to suit every palate, and you may soon find that you have joined the ranks of millions of curry addicts around the world.

healthy favourites

Unfortunately, many curries contain a lot of oil, butter and cream, which are blended with herbs and spices to give rich but unhealthy dishes. The delicious recipes in this book will show you that you can cook healthy curries without compromising on flavour and taste.

We have re-created your favourite curries – and some more unusual ones – without relying on unhealthy ingredients. We use these in much smaller quantities than usual and replace them with healthier options, like groundnut oil, which is much lower in saturated fat than ghee, sunflower oil or butter. We have used fat-free natural yogurt and reduced-fat coconut milk instead of cream and butter.

We have also omitted or reduced sugar and replaced it with agave syrup. Sweeter than honey, this organic, fat-free sweetener can replace sugar in many recipes – you only need a very small amount. Likewise, when seasoning your dishes, be sure to use salt sparingly, as a high intake can contribute to high blood pressure and heart disease.

basic ingredients

You can buy most of the ingredients you need for the recipes in this book in any large supermarket. Markets and ethnic food shops are great places to find the more unusual items, and they will stock large packets of spices at good prices. You can also order 'exotic' ingredients from specialist websites and have them delivered to your door.

dry spices

The flavour of dry spices decreases with time, so buy them in small quantities and use them up quickly for best results.

amchoor

Dried mango powder, used as a souring agent in Indian curries. Substitute with a little lemon juice or tamarind paste if unavailable.

asafoetida

Also known as devil's dung, this plant resin can be bought in a lump or dried and ground in powder form. It is very strong in flavour. Usually used in tiny amounts in lentil dishes, it is believed to counteract flatulence.

cardamom

This is usually used whole, in its pod, as an aromatic to flavour rice and curries. You can also use the little black seeds inside the pods on their own, by crushing them and using as part of a spice mixture or for a garam masala.

cassia

Also known as Chinese cinnamon, cassia is an aromatic tree bark, which can be bought as sticks, rolled bark or in powder form. It has a coarser texture and stronger flavour than cinnamon does.

chilli
Whole dried red chillies add the fiery heat to a curry. Dried chilli flakes tend to have a milder flavour and chilli powders made from ground dried chillies vary in heat, ranging from mild or medium to hot.

cinnamon
This sweet and warming aromatic spice comes from the bark of a tree and is available as sticks or rolled bark. It is also widely used in ground powder form.

cloves
These aromatic dried buds from an evergreen tree can be used whole or ground to a powder.

coriander seeds
The small, pale brown seeds of the coriander plant have a fresh, citrus flavour. Available whole or ground, they form the base of many curry pastes and dry spice mixes.

cumin
Essential in Asian cooking, these small elongated brown seeds are used whole or ground, and have a distinctive, warm, pungent aroma. Whole seeds may be dry-roasted and sprinkled over a dish just before serving.

curry powders
Ready-made curry powders are widely available and there are many different varieties, depending on the spice mix. Some are simply labelled as mild, medium or hot, but there are many specific mixes, such as Tandoori Spice Mix or Madras Curry Powder.

fennel seeds
These small, pale green seeds have a subtle aniseed flavour and are used as a flavouring in some spice mixes.

fenugreek seeds
Usually square in shape, these tiny, shiny yellow seeds are used widely in pickles and ground into spice mixes for curries.

garam masala
This common spice mix is usually added to a dish at the end of cooking time. A classic garam masala mix comprises cardamom, cloves, cumin, peppercorns, cinnamon and nutmeg. See page 80 for recipe.

mustard seeds
Black, brown or yellow, these tiny round seeds are widely used as a flavouring to dishes and are usually fried in oil until they 'pop' to impart a mellow, nutty flavour.

nigella seeds
Also known as black onion seeds or *kalonji*, these tiny, matt black, oval seeds are most frequently used to flavour breads and pickles.

saffron
These deep orange strands are the dried stamens from a particular type of crocus and are used to give rice dishes and desserts a musky fragrance and golden colour.

star anise
These dark brown, flower-shaped seed pods have a decidedly aniseed-like flavour.

turmeric
This bright yellow-orange rhizome is widely available as a dried, ground powder. Turmeric has a warm, musky flavour and is used in small quantities to add flavour and colour to lentil and rice dishes and curries.

fresh herbs & aromatics

chillies
Fresh green and red chillies are used in many types of curries to give heat and flavour. Much of the heat resides in the pith and seeds, so if you want to enjoy the chilli taste with less heat, make a long slit down the length of the chilli and carefully scrape out and discard the pith and seeds before slicing or chopping the flesh.

coriander
The parsley of the East, fresh coriander is used widely in Asian cooking. Often the delicate leaves are used to flavour dishes, but the stalks and roots can also be used, especially in Thai curry pastes.

curry leaves
These highly aromatic leaves are used fresh in Indian and Southeast Asian cooking. They come attached to stalks in sprays and are pulled off the stalks before use. Fresh curry leaves freeze very well and can be used straight from the freezer.

galangal
This rhizome is used in savoury dishes in the same way as its cousin, ginger. It is peeled and cut into very fine slivers or finely chopped. You can use fresh root ginger instead if you can't find any galangal.

garlic
One of the essential flavours used in cooking all over the world, garlic cooked with ginger and onion forms the base of many curries. It is used sliced, crushed or grated.

ginger
Another indispensable aromatic, fresh root ginger has a fresh, peppery flavour and is used in both savoury and sweet dishes.

kaffir lime leaves
The leaves from the knobbly kaffir lime are

highly aromatic. When used in a curry, they are usually finely shredded but are sometimes left whole. They freeze very well and can be used straight from the freezer.

lemon grass

Known as *sere* in Indonesia, *serai* in Malaysia, *takrai* in Thailand and *tanglad* in the Phillipines, this green grass is used for its citrus flavour and aroma. It can be used whole by bruising the base of the stalk, or can be finely sliced or chopped. Remove the tough outer leaves before slicing or chopping, as they can be very fibrous.

onions

This humble vegetable forms the base of many curries. Sliced or chopped, it is usually slowly fried before the other ingredients are added. Store onions in a wire basket in the kitchen at room temperature.

shallots

These small, sweet and pungent members of the onion family are widely used in Southeast Asian cooking. To peel them, slice them in half and only then remove the outer skin.

Thai basil

Found in Oriental food shops, this delicate herb is used to garnish and flavour curries. You can substitute regular basil if you cannot find any.

other useful ingredients

coconut milk & coconut cream

Widely used in Asian cooking, canned coconut milk is readily available. It is added to curries to impart a rich, creamy texture. For a healthier option, use reduced-fat coconut milk. Coconut cream is a thicker, richer version.

gram flour

Also known as *besan*, this pale yellow flour, made from dried chickpeas, is used widely for thickening and binding, as well as being the main ingredient in savoury batters.

palm sugar

Known as *jaggery* in India and *nam tan peep* in Thailand, this is the sugar produced from the sap of various kinds of palms. Sold in cakes or cans, palm sugar has a deep, caramel flavour and is light brown in colour. It is used in curries to balance the spices. You can use any brown sugar as a substitute.

shrimp paste

Also known as *kapee*, this is a pungent preserve used in Asian cooking. Made by pounding shrimp with salt and leaving it to decompose, it has a powerful aroma, which disappears when cooked.

sweet chilli sauce

This sweet and mild sauce is made from red chillies, sugar, garlic and vinegar.

tamarind paste

Used as a souring agent in curries, the paste from the tamarind pod can be used straight from the jar. You can also buy it in semi-dried pulp form, which needs to be soaked in warm water and strained before use.

Thai fish sauce

Also known as *nam pla*, this sauce is made from the liquid extracted from salted, fermented fish and is one of the main ingredients in Thai cooking.

recipes
under 200
calories

mandarin & lychee frappé

Calories per serving **68**
Makes **150 ml (¼ pint)**

100 g (3½ oz) **mandarin oranges**, canned in natural juice
50 g (2 oz) **lychees**, canned in natural juice
ice cubes

Put the oranges and lychees and the juices from the cans into a food processor or blender, add the ice cubes and process briefly.

Pour the frappé into glasses and serve immediately.

For ruby smoothie, put the juice of 2 oranges and 1 apple in a food processor or blender with 150 g (5 oz) each raspberries and strawberries. Add 150 ml (¼ pint) low fat yogurt and process briefly.
Calories per serving 241

seafood with chillies

Calories per serving **174**
Serves **4**
Preparation time **5 minutes**
Cooking time **about 10 minutes**

1½ tablespoons **sunflower oil**
3–4 **garlic cloves**, finely chopped
125 g (4 oz) **red pepper**, deseeded and cut into bite-sized pieces
1 **small onion**, cut into eighths
1 **carrot**, cut into matchsticks
450 g (14½ oz) **prepared mixed seafood**, such as prawns, squid, small scallops
2.5 cm (1 inch) piece of **fresh root ginger**, peeled and finely grated
2 tablespoons **vegetable or seafood stock**
1 tablespoon **oyster sauce**
½ tablespoon **light soy sauce**
1 **long fresh red chilli**, stemmed, deseeded and sliced diagonally
1–2 **spring onions**, finely sliced

Heat the oil in a nonstick wok or frying pan and stir-fry the garlic over medium heat until it is lightly browned.

Add the red pepper, onion and carrot and stir-fry for 2 minutes.

Add all the seafood together with the ginger, stock, oyster sauce and soy sauce and stir-fry for 2–3 minutes or until the prawns turn pink and all the seafood is cooked.

Add the chilli and spring onions and mix well together. Spoon on to a serving plate and serve immediately, with rice, if liked.

For seafood with pineapple sweet chilli, stir-fry the red pepper, onion and carrot after the garlic has lightly browned. Add all the seafood, ginger, stock, oyster sauce and 2–3 tablespoons pineapple-flavoured sweet chilli sauce (or plain if the flavoured version is unavailable). Omit the spring onion and add a handful of Thai basil leaves with the chilli, lightly toss together for a minute to combine before serving. **Calories per serving 209**

malaysian spicy cauliflower

Calories per serving **118**
Serves **4**
Preparation time **10 minutes**
Cooking time **10 minutes**

2 tablespoons **groundnut oil**
1 **fresh red chilli**, deseeded
   and finely chopped
1 **onion**, thickly sliced
2 **garlic cloves**, chopped
1 teaspoon **salt**
500g (1 lb) **cauliflower**, cut
   into florets then sliced

Heat the oil in a wok over a high heat until the oil starts to shimmer. Add the chilli, onion and garlic and stir-fry for 1 minute.

Add the salt and cauliflower. Stir well to combine all the flavours then sprinkle with 3 tablespoons water, cover and steam for 3–4 minutes, until tender.

For spicy cauliflower soup, start the recipe as above, adding 250 g (8 oz) peeled and diced floury potatoes with the cauliflower. Once all the flavours are tossed together, pour in 1 litre (1¾ pints) vegetable stock. Simmer for 15 minutes, then blend until smooth. Serve with a drizzle of chilli oil. **Calories per serving 186**

watermelon cooler

Calories per serving **101**
Makes **300 ml (½ pint)**

100 g (3½ oz) **watermelon**
100 g (3½ oz) **strawberries**
100 ml (3½ fl oz) **water**
small handful of **mint** or
  tarragon leaves, plus extra
  to serve (optional)

Skin and deseed the watermelon and chop the flesh into cubes. Hull the strawberries. Freeze the melon and strawberries until solid.

Put the frozen melon and strawberries in a food processor or blender, add the water and the mint or tarragon and process until smooth.

Pour the mixture into 2 short glasses, decorate with mint or tarragon leaves, if liked, and serve immediately.

For melon & almond smoothie, process 100 g (3½ oz) frozen galia melon flesh with 100 ml (3½ fl oz) sweetened, chilled almond milk. **Calories per serving 48**

gujarati carrot salad

Calories per serving **104**
Serves **4**
Preparation time **10 minutes**
Cooking time **2–3 minutes**

500 g (1 lb) **carrots**, coarsely
  grated
4 tablespoons **lemon juice**
1 tablespoon **clear honey**
1 tablespoon **vegetable oil**
½ teaspoon **dried chilli flakes**
2 teaspoons **black mustard
  seeds**
4 **curry leaves**
salt

Put the carrots into a serving bowl. Mix the lemon juice and honey together and pour over the carrots. Season with salt.

Heat the oil in a small saucepan and add the chilli flakes, mustard seeds and curry leaves. As soon as the mustard seeds start to pop, remove the saucepan from the heat and pour the dressing over the carrots. Stir well to mix.

For beetroot & carrot salad, replace 250 g (8 oz) of the coarsely grated carrots with 250 g (8 oz) peeled and coarsely grated freshly cooked beetroot and proceed as above. **Calories per serving 118**

cabbage bhaji

Calories per serving **110**
Serves **4**
Preparation time **10 minutes**
Cooking time **10 minutes**

500 g (1 lb) **white cabbage**,
   roughly chopped
150 ml (¼ pint) **boiling water**
1 tablespoon **vegetable oil**
2 teaspoons **urad dhal** (dried
   lentils)
1 teaspoon **black mustard
   seeds**
1 **dried red chilli**, finely
   chopped
6–8 **curry leaves**
2 tablespoons **grated fresh
   coconut**
salt and **pepper**

Put the cabbage into a large saucepan with the water, cover and cook over a medium heat for 10 minutes, stirring occasionally. Drain, return to the pan, set aside and keep warm.

Meanwhile, heat the oil in a small nonstick frying pan and add the urad dhal, mustard seeds and chilli. Stir-fry for 1–2 minutes, and when the dhal turns light brown add the curry leaves. Fry, stirring constantly, for 2 minutes.

Pour the spiced oil over the cabbage, stir in the coconut, season with salt and pepper and serve hot.

For mild-spiced cabbage bhaji, heat a small saucepan, then add 1–2 tablespoons vegetable oil. When hot add 1 tablespoon cumin seeds, 2 garlic cloves, thinly sliced, and 1 teaspoon chopped ginger. Stir-fry for 1–2 minutes, then pour the oil over the prepared cabbage, as above. Season and serve hot.
Calories per serving 112

spicy fish

Calories per serving **113**
Serves **2**
Preparation time **10 minutes,
plus marinating**
Cooking time **5 minutes**

1 **garlic clove**, peeled
2 **red shallots**, chopped
1 **lemon grass stalk**
½ teaspoon **ground turmeric**
½ teaspoon **ground ginger**
1 **mild fresh red chilli**,
    deseeded and roughly
    chopped
1 tablespoon **groundnut oil**
2 teaspoon **fish sauce**
300 g (10 oz) **boneless
white fish fillets**, cut into
    bite-sized pieces
salt and **pepper**
1 tablespoon chopped **fresh
    coriander**, to garnish

Put the garlic, shallots, lemon grass, turmeric, ginger, chilli and salt and pepper into a food processor or blender and process until a paste is formed, adding the oil and fish sauce to help the grinding.

Place the fish in a bowl and toss with the spice paste. Cover and refrigerate for 15 minutes.

Thread the pieces of fish on to skewers and arrange on a foil-lined tray. Cook under a preheated hot grill for 4–5 minutes, turning once so that the pieces brown evenly. Serve sprinkled with the coriander.

For Chinese greens to serve as an accompaniment, put 300 g (10 oz) raw shredded Chinese greens in a saucepan of boiling water and cook for 1–2 minutes. Drain and place on warmed serving plates. Heat 1 teaspoon groundnut oil in a small pan and cook ½ teaspoon finely chopped garlic briefly. Stir in 1 teaspoon oyster sauce, 1 tablespoon water and ½ tablespoon sesame oil, then bring to the boil. Pour over the greens and toss together. **Calories per serving 35**

trivandrum beetroot curry

Calories per serving **122**
Serves **4**
Preparation time **15 minutes**
Cooking time **25–30 minutes**

1 tablespoon **groundnut oil**
1 teaspoon **black mustard seeds**
1 **onion**, chopped
2 **garlic cloves**, chopped
2 **fresh red chillies**, deseeded and finely chopped
8 **curry leaves**
1 teaspoon **ground turmeric**
1 teaspoon **cumin seeds**
1 **cinnamon stick**
400 g (13 oz) **raw beetroot**, peeled and cut into matchsticks
200 g (7 oz) canned **chopped tomatoes**
250 ml (8 fl oz) **water**
100 ml (3½ fl oz) **reduced-fat coconut milk**
juice of 1 **lime**
salt
chopped **fresh coriander leaves**, to garnish

Heat the oil in a wok or saucepan over a medium heat. Add the mustard seeds and as soon as they begin to 'pop' (after a few seconds), add the onion, garlic and chillies. Cook for about 5 minutes until the onion is soft and translucent.

Add the remaining spices and the beetroot. Fry for a further 1–2 minutes, then add the tomatoes, measured water and a pinch of salt. Simmer for 15–20 minutes, stirring occasionally, until the beetroot is tender.

Stir in the coconut milk and simmer for a further 1–2 minutes until the sauce has thickened. Stir in the lime juice and check the seasoning. Garnish with chopped coriander and serve immediately.

For spiced beetroot salad, thickly slice 625 g (1 ¼ lb) cooked beetroot and arrange on a wide serving platter with 1 very thinly sliced red onion and a large handful of rocket leaves. Make a dressing by whisking 200 ml (7 fl oz) reduced-fat coconut milk with 1 tablespoon curry powder and 4 tablespoons each of very finely chopped coriander and mint. Season to taste and drizzle over the beetroot salad. Toss to mix well and serve.
Calories per serving 120

coconut, carrot & spinach salad

Calories per serving **129**
Serves **4**
Preparation time **10 minutes**
Cooking time **1 minute**

300 g (10 oz) **baby spinach**,
  finely chopped
1 **carrot**, coarsely grated
25 g (1 oz) **fresh coconut**,
  grated
2 tablespoons **groundnut oil**
2 teaspoons **black mustard
  seeds**
1 teaspoon **cumin seeds**
juice of 1 **lime**
juice of 1 **orange**
salt and **pepper**

Place the spinach in a large bowl with the carrot and coconut, and toss together lightly.

Heat the oil a small frying pan over a medium heat. Add the mustard and cumin seeds, and stir-fry for 20–30 seconds until fragrant and the mustard seeds start to 'pop'.

Remove from the heat, and pour over the salad with the lime and orange juice. Season well and toss before serving.

For spicy coconut, carrot & spinach sauté, heat 1 tablespoon groundnut oil in a large wok or frying pan and add 1 finely diced red chilli, 2 finely chopped garlic cloves, 4 finely sliced spring onions and 1 teaspoon each of cumin and black mustard seeds. Stir-fry for 1 minute, then add 1 coarsely grated carrot. Stir-fry for 2–3 minutes and add 200 g (7 oz) baby spinach. Stir-fry over a high heat for 2–3 minutes or until the spinach has just wilted. Season, sprinkle with 25 g (1 oz) grated fresh coconut and serve immediately. **Calories per serving 90**

carrot & red cabbage slaw

Calories per serving **137**
Serves **4**
Preparation time **10 minutes**
Cooking time **1 minute**

3 large **carrots**, coarsely
  grated
300 g (10 oz) **red cabbage**,
  finely shredded
juice of **2 limes**
2 teaspoons **agave syrup**
2 tablespoons **light olive oil**
1 **fresh red chilli**, finely diced
1 tablespoon **black mustard
  seeds**
salt and **pepper**

Place the carrots and red cabbage in a large bowl. Mix together the lime juice and agave syrup, and stir into the vegetables. Toss to mix well, and set aside.

Heat the oil in a small frying pan over a medium heat. Add the chilli and mustard seeds, and stir-fry for 20–30 seconds until fragrant and the mustard seeds start to 'pop'.

Scrape the contents of the frying pan over the salad, season well and toss to combine. Serve immediately.

For toasted spiced chapati wedges, to serve as an accompaniment, cut 4 ready-made chapatis into wedges and arrange on 2 large baking sheets. Lightly spray with cooking oil spray and sprinkle over 1 tablespoon crushed cumin seeds, 1 tablespoon nigella seeds, 2 teaspoons mild chilli powder and a little sea salt. Cook in a preheated oven at 180°C (350°F), Gas Mark 4, for 8–10 minutes or until crisp. Serve hot. **Calories per serving 255**

cucumber lassi

Calories per serving **140**
Makes **400 ml (14 fl oz)**

150 g (5 oz) **cucumber**
150 g (5 oz) **live natural
  yogurt**
100 ml (3½ fl oz) ice-cold
  still water
handful of **mint**
½ teaspoon **ground cumin**
squeeze of **lemon juice**

Peel and roughly chop the cucumber. Place in a food processor or blender and add the yogurt and iced water.

Pull the mint leaves off their stalks, reserving a few for decoration. Chop the remainder roughly and put them into the food processor. Add the cumin and lemon juice and process briefly.

Pour the smoothie into a tall glass, decorate with mint leaves, if liked, and serve immediately.

For mango lassi, cut the flesh of a mango into cubes and add it to a food processor or blender with 150 ml (¼ pint) live natural yogurt and the same amount of ice-cold still water, 1 tablespoon rosewater and ¼ teaspoon ground cardamom. Process briefly and serve. **Calories per serving 276**

peanut & cucumber salad

Calories per serving **147**
Serves **4**
Preparation time **5 minutes**
Cooking time **5 minutes**

1 large **cucumber**, peeled and
finely chopped
4 tablespoons **lemon juice**
1 tablespoon **light olive oil**
1 teaspoon **yellow mustard
seeds**
2 teaspoons **black mustard
seeds**
8–10 **curry leaves**
1–2 **fresh red chillies**,
deseeded and finely
chopped
4 tablespoons finely chopped
roasted peanuts
salt and **pepper**

Place the cucumber in a large bowl, sprinkle over the
lemon juice and season with salt. Stir to mix well and
set aside.

Heat the oil in a small frying pan over a medium heat.
Add the mustard seeds, curry leaves and chilli, and
stir-fry for 1–2 minutes until fragrant and the mustard
seeds start to 'pop'.

Add the contents of the pan to the cucumber mixture.
Toss to mix well, sprinkle over the chopped peanuts and
serve immediately.

For spicy roasted tomato salad, cut 10 midi plum
tomatoes in half and place on a baking sheet, cut side
up. Season and sprinkle over 1 tablespoon mild curry
powder and 2 teaspoons cumin seeds. Lightly spray
with cooking oil spray and roast in a preheated oven at
200°C (400°F), Gas Mark 6, for 12–15 minutes. Allow
to cool. Arrange 200 g (7 oz) mixed salad leaves on a
wide serving platter with ½ sliced red onion. Arrange
the cooled tomatoes over the salad, squeeze over the
juice of 2 limes and sprinkle with 4 tablespoons toasted
pumpkin seeds. **Calories per serving 133**

green masala chicken kebabs

Calories per serving **148**
Serves **4**
Preparation time **10 minutes,
plus marinating**
Cooking time **10 minutes**

4 boneless, skinless **chicken
breast fillets**, cubed
juice of **1 lime**
100 ml (3½ fl oz) **fat-free
natural yogurt**
1 teaspoon peeled and finely
grated **fresh root ginger**
1 **garlic clove**, crushed
1 **fresh green chilli**, deseeded
and chopped
large handful of finely chopped
fresh coriander leaves
large handful of finely chopped
mint leaves
1 tablespoon **medium curry
powder**
pinch of **salt**
lime wedges, to serve

Place the chicken in a large bowl. Place all the remaining ingredients in a food processor and blend until smooth, adding a little water if necessary. Pour over the chicken, and toss to mix well. Cover and leave to marinate in the refrigerator overnight.

Preheat the grill until hot. Thread the chicken on to 8 metal skewers, and grill for 6–8 minutes, turning once or twice, until the chicken is cooked through. Serve immediately with lime wedges for squeezing.

For red masala chicken kebabs, mix 4 tablespoons fat-free natural yogurt with 4 tablespoons tomato purée, 1 teaspoon grated ginger, 4 crushed garlic cloves, 1 tablespoon chilli powder, 1 teaspoon ground cumin and 1 teaspoon turmeric. Pour over the chicken and marinate and cook as above. **Calories per serving 152**

dry prawn curry

Calories per serving **157**
Serves **4**
Preparation time **10 minutes**
Cooking time **10 minutes**

1 **onion**, roughly chopped
4 **garlic cloves**, chopped
8 tablespoons **lemon juice**
1 teaspoon peeled and finely
   grated **fresh root ginger**
1 teaspoon **ground turmeric**
½ teaspoon **chilli powder**
2 teaspoons shop-bought
   medium curry paste
1 tablespoon **groundnut oil**
500 g (1 lb) **raw tiger prawns**,
   peeled and deveined
4 tablespoons chopped **fresh**
   coriander leaves
4 **spring onions**, finely sliced
salt

Place the onion, garlic, lemon juice, ginger, turmeric, chilli powder and curry paste in a food processor and blend until fairly smooth. Season with salt.

Heat the oil in a wide saucepan over a medium heat. Add the onion paste and stir-fry for 2–3 minutes. Add the prawns and stir-fry for a further 4–5 minutes until they turn pink and are cooked through.

Remove from the heat and stir in the coriander and spring onions. Serve immediately.

For lemon & herbed couscous, to serve as an accompaniment, place 300 g (10 oz) couscous in a shallow heatproof bowl. Add boiling water to just cover the couscous, cover tightly and allow to stand for 12–15 minutes. Fluff up the grains of the couscous with a fork, season and stir in a large handful each of chopped coriander and mint. Squeeze over the juice of 1 lemon and serve immediately. **Calories per serving 260**

tamarind & date chutney

Calories per serving **161**
Serves **4**
Preparation time **10 minutes**

200 g (7 oz) **stoned dried
dates**, roughly chopped
1 tablespoon **tamarind paste**
1 teaspoon **ground cumin**
1 teaspoon **chilli powder**
1 tablespoon **tomato ketchup**
200 ml (7 fl oz) **water**
salt

Put all the ingredients into a food processor or blender and process until fairly smooth.

Transfer the mixture to a serving bowl, cover and chill until required. The chutney will keep for up to 3 days in the refrigerator.

For chutney-marinated paneer, spoon the chutney over 250 g (8 oz) paneer, cubed, and leave to marinate for several hours. Drain well. Cover the grill shelf with foil and brush with oil. Spread out the paneer on the foil and cook under a preheated hot grill until browned, turning as necessary. **Calories per serving 368**

spiced beetroot

Calories per serving **182**
Serves **4**
Preparation time **10 minutes**
Cooking time **5–6 minutes**

1 tablespoon **vegetable oil**
2 **garlic cloves**, finely chopped
1 teaspoon grated **fresh root ginger**
1 teaspoon **cumin seeds**
1 teaspoon **coriander seeds**, crushed
½ teaspoon **dried red chilli flakes**
625 g (1 ¼ lb) freshly cooked and peeled **beetroot**, cut into wedges
150 ml (¼ pint) **coconut milk**
¼ teaspoon **ground cardamom seeds**
grated rind and juice of 1 **lime**
handful of chopped **fresh coriander**
salt and **pepper**

Heat the oil in a large frying pan and add the garlic, ginger, cumin seeds, coriander seeds and chilli flakes. Stir-fry for 1–2 minutes, then add the beetroot. Fry, stirring gently, for 1 minute, then add the coconut milk, cardamom and lime rind and juice. Cook over a medium heat for 2–3 minutes.

Stir in the fresh coriander, season with salt and pepper and serve hot, warm or at room temperature.

For spiced mixed vegetables, replace the beetroot with 250 g (8 oz) cooked baby carrots (or chunks of large carrots), 250 g (8 oz) cooked swede, cut into cubes, and 250 g (8 oz) cooked parsnip, thickly sliced. **Calories per serving 174**

coconut & coriander mussels

Calories per serving **185**
Serves **4**
Preparation time **10 minutes**
Cooking time **15 minutes**

1 tablespoon **vegetable oil**
4 **spring onions**, finely
  chopped
2.5 cm (1 inch) length **galangal**
  or **fresh root ginger**,
  shredded
1 **fresh green chilli**, finely
  chopped
200 ml (7 fl oz) can **reduced-
  fat coconut milk**
large bunch of **fresh coriander**,
  chopped, plus extra to
  garnish
1 tablespoon chopped **Thai
  basil** (optional)
200 ml (7 fl oz) **fish stock**
2 tablespoons **Thai fish sauce**
2 tablespoons **lime juice**
1 tablespoon **soy sauce**
1 tablespoon **soft brown
  sugar**
3–4 **lime leaves**, shredded
  (optional)
1 kg (2 lb) **mussels**, scrubbed
  and debearded
desiccated coconut, toasted,
  to garnish (optional)

Heat the oil in a large saucepan and cook the spring onions, galangal or ginger and chilli for 2 minutes until soft. Add the remaining ingredients except the mussels and warm gently until the sugar has dissolved. Turn up the heat and bring up to boiling point, then reduce the heat and simmer gently for 5 minutes to allow the flavours to develop.

Tip the mussels into the coconut sauce and cover with a tight-fitting lid. Cook for 3–4 minutes or until the mussels have opened – discard any that have not.

Spoon into serving bowls with plenty of the juices and sprinkle with extra coriander leaves and desiccated coconut, if using. Serve immediately.

For coconut & coriander seafood with lime rice, replace the mussels with 500 g (1 lb) fresh or frozen prepared seafood mix and cook as above, but omitting the lime leaves. Cook 200 g (7 oz) rice with the grated rind of 1 lime. Serve the rice in bowls and ladle over the seafood. **Calories per serving 484**

warm cabbage salad

Calories per serving **188**
Serves **4**
Preparation time **10 minutes**
Cooking time **5–7 minutes**

2 tablespoons **sunflower oil**
2 teaspoons **black mustard seeds**
1 tablespoon finely grated **fresh root ginger**
10–12 **curry leaves**
1 small **white cabbage,** halved, cored and finely shredded
2–3 tablespoons **grated fresh coconut**
salt and **pepper**
2 tablespoons **chopped roasted peanuts**, to garnish

Heat the oil in a large frying pan or wok and add the mustard seeds. When they start to pop, add the ginger, curry leaves and cabbage and stir-fry over a high heat for 4–5 minutes.

Add the grated coconut and stir-fry for a further 1–2 minutes. Season well, garnish with the roasted peanuts and serve immediately.

For sweet fennel & cabbage salad, use ½ small white cabbage, halved, cored and finely shredded, 1 head fennel, finely shredded, and 1 large carrot, peeled and coarsely grated. Add these to the pan with the ginger and curry leaves. Proceed as above.
Calories per serving 192

okra, pea & tomato curry

Calories per serving **188**
Serves **4**
Preparation time **5 minutes**
Cooking time **about
20 minutes**

1 tablespoon **groundnut oil**
6–8 **curry leaves**
2 teaspoons **black mustard
seeds**
1 **onion**, finely diced
2 teaspoons **ground cumin**
1 teaspoon **ground coriander**
2 teaspoons **curry powder**
1 teaspoon **ground turmeric**
3 **garlic cloves**, finely chopped
500 g (1 lb) **okra**, cut on the
diagonal into 2.5 cm (1 inch)
pieces
200 g (7 oz) **fresh** or **frozen
peas**
2 ripe **plum tomatoes**, finely
chopped
salt and **pepper**
3 tablespoons **grated fresh
coconut**, to serve

Heat the oil in a large nonstick wok or frying pan over a medium heat. Add the curry leaves, mustard seeds and onion. Stir-fry for 3–4 minutes until fragrant and the onion is starting to soften, then add the cumin, coriander, curry powder and turmeric. Stir-fry for a further 1–2 minutes until fragrant.

Add the garlic and okra, and increase the heat to high. Cook, stirring, for 2–3 minutes, then add the peas and tomatoes. Season to taste, cover and reduce the heat to low. Cook gently for 10–12 minutes, stirring occasionally, until the okra is just tender. Remove from the heat and sprinkle over the grated coconut just before serving.

For spiced seeded pea & tomato pilaf, place 300 g (10 oz) basmati rice in a medium saucepan with 2 teaspoons dry-roasted cumin seeds, 1 tablespoon crushed dry-roasted coriander seeds, 2 teaspoons black mustard seeds, 200 g (7 oz) fresh or frozen peas and 3 peeled, deseeded and finely chopped tomatoes. Add 650 ml (1 pint 2 fl oz) boiling vegetable stock, bring to the boil and season to taste. Reduce the heat to low, cover the pan and cook gently for 10–12 minutes or until all the liquid has been absorbed. Remove from the heat and allow to stand, covered and undisturbed, for 10–15 minutes. Fluff up the grains with a fork and serve. **Calories per serving 343**

cauliflower & chickpea curry

Calories per serving **194**
(not including mint raita)
Serves **4**
Preparation time **10 minutes**
Cooking time **about 20 minutes**

1 tablespoon **groundnut oil**
8 **spring onions,** cut into 5 cm
(2 inch) lengths
2 teaspoons grated **garlic**
2 teaspoons **ground ginger**
2 tablespoons **medium curry
powder**
300 g (10 oz) **cauliflower
florets**
1 **red pepper,** cored,
deseeded and diced
1 **yellow pepper,** cored,
deseeded and diced
400 g (13 oz) can **chopped
tomatoes**
400 g (13 oz) can **chickpeas,**
rinsed and drained
salt and **pepper**

Heat the oil in a large nonstick frying pan over a
medium heat. Add the spring onions and stir-fry for
2–3 minutes. Add the garlic, ginger and curry powder,
and stir-fry for 20–30 seconds until fragrant. Now add
the cauliflower and peppers, and stir-fry for a further
2–3 minutes.

Stir in the tomatoes and bring to the boil. Cover, reduce
the heat to medium and simmer for 10 minutes, stirring
occasionally. Add the chickpeas, season to taste and
bring back to the boil. Remove from the heat and serve
immediately with mint raita, if liked.

For broccoli & black-eye bean curry, follow the
recipe above replacing the cauliflower with 300 g
(10 oz) broccoli florets and the chickpeas with a 400 g
(13 oz) can black-eye beans. **Calories per serving 193**

mulligatawny soup

Calories per serving **197**
Serves **4**
Preparation time **15 minutes**
Cooking time **50 minutes**

50 g (2 oz) **butter**
1 large **onion**, thinly sliced
1 small **carrot**, cut into small
  dice
1 large **celery stick**, finely
  chopped
25 g (1 oz) **flour**
2 teaspoons **curry powder**
900 ml (1½ pints) **vegetable
  stock**
1 large **cooking apple**
2 teaspoons **lemon juice**
25 g (1 oz) cooked **basmati
  rice**
fresh **flat leaf parsley leaves**,
  roughly chopped, to garnish

Melt the butter in a saucepan and gently fry the onion, carrot and celery until soft. Do not allow to brown. Stir in the flour and curry powder. Cook for 2 minutes and pour in the stock.

Bring to the boil, stirring constantly. Reduce the heat, cover with a lid and simmer gently for 30 minutes, stirring occasionally.

Peel, core and dice the apple, then add to the soup with the lemon juice and rice. Season to taste and simmer for a further 10 minutes. Serve hot garnished with a sprinkling of parsley.

For lamb mulligatawny, cut 500 g (1 lb) boneless shoulder or leg of lamb into bite-sized pieces. Lightly brown the meat for 3–5 minutes before adding the onion, carrot and celery. Proceed as above, but increase the cooking time to 45 minutes or longer, until the lamb is tender, before adding the apples. **Calories per serving 344**

recipes
under 300
calories

south indian vegetable stew

Calories per serving **200**
Serves **4**
Preparation time **15 minutes**
Cooking time **20–25 minutes**

1 tablespoon **groundnut oil**
6 **shallots**, halved and thinly
 sliced
2 teaspoons **black mustard
 seeds**
8–10 **curry leaves**
1 **fresh green chilli**, thinly
 sliced
2 teaspoons peeled and finely
 grated **fresh root ginger**
1 teaspoon **ground turmeric**
2 teaspoons **ground cumin**
6 **black peppercorns**
2 **carrots,** cut into thick batons
1 **courgette**, cut into thick
 batons
200 g (7 oz) **French beans**,
 trimmed
1 **potato**, peeled and cut into
 thin batons
400 ml (14 fl oz) can **reduced-
 fat coconut milk**
400 ml (14 fl oz) **vegetable
 stock**
2 tablespoons **lemon juice**
salt and **pepper**

Heat the oil in a large frying pan over a medium heat. Add the shallots and stir-fry for 4–5 minutes. Add the mustard seeds, curry leaves, chilli, ginger, turmeric, cumin and peppercorns, and stir-fry for a further 1–2 minutes until fragrant.

Add the carrots, courgette, beans and potato to the pan. Pour in the coconut milk and stock and bring to the boil. Reduce the heat to low, cover and simmer gently for 12–15 minutes until the vegetables are tender. Season to taste, remove from the heat and squeeze over the lemon juice just before serving.

For spicy tomato, vegetable & coconut curry, follow the recipe above, replacing the turmeric, cumin and black peppercorns with 2 tablespoons hot curry powder, and the vegetable stock with 400 ml (14 fl oz) tomato passata. **Calories per serving 231**

whole pomfret in banana leaf

Calories per serving **206**
Serves **4**
Preparation time **20 minutes**
Cooking time **15–20 minutes**

1 large **pomfret**, gutted and
   cleaned
1 **banana leaf**, large enough
   to wrap the fish in
5 cm (2 inch) piece of **fresh
   root ginger**, peeled and cut
   into matchsticks
50 ml (2 fl oz) **coconut cream**
6 tablespoons chopped **fresh
   coriander**
6 tablespoons chopped **mint**
6 tablespoons **lime juice**
3 **spring onions**, finely sliced
4 **lime leaves**, finely shredded
2 **fresh red chillies**, deseeded
   and finely sliced
salt and **pepper**

Use a small sharp knife to score the fish flesh
diagonally on both sides. Dip the banana leaf into
boiling water for 15–20 seconds to make it supple and
pliable for wrapping the fish. Remove and rinse under
cold water. Dry with kitchen paper.

Mix together the ginger, coconut cream, chopped herbs,
lime juice, spring onions, lime leaves and chilli in a bowl.
Season the mixture to taste.

Lay the banana leaf on a work surface and place the
pomfret in the centre. Spread the herb mixture over
the pomfret and wrap in the leaf to form a neat parcel.
Secure with bamboo skewers or cocktail sticks.

Place the parcel in a large bamboo steamer and
steam, covered, over a wok of simmering water for
15–20 minutes or until the fish is cooked through.

For stuffed spicy trout, divide the herb mix among
4 cleaned trout, placing it in the body cavities. Allow to
marinate for 30 minutes, then bake in an ovenproof dish
at 190°C (375°F), Gas Mark 5, for about 30 minutes,
until cooked and aromatic. **Calories per serving 256**

green curry with straw mushrooms

Calories per serving **225**
Serves **4**
Preparation time **10 minutes**
Cooking time **10 minutes**

300 ml (½ pint) **coconut milk**,
plus extra for drizzling
40 g (1½ oz) **green curry
paste**
300 ml (½ pint) **vegetable
stock**
2 **aubergines**, roughly
chopped into large chunks
40 g (1½ oz) **soft brown
sugar**
4 teaspoons **soy sauce**
25 g (1 oz) **fresh root ginger**,
peeled and finely chopped
425 g (14 oz) can **straw
mushrooms**, drained
50 g (2 oz) **green pepper**,
cored, deseeded and
thinly sliced
salt

Put most of the coconut milk and the curry paste in a
saucepan over a medium heat and stir well. Pour in the
stock, then add the aubergines, sugar, soy sauce, ginger
and salt to taste.

Bring to the boil and cook, stirring, for 5 minutes. Add
the mushrooms and green pepper, reduce the heat and
cook for 2 minutes until piping hot.

Serve in bowls, drizzled with a little extra coconut milk.

For vegetable korma, heat 1 tablespoon vegetable
oil in a large saucepan, add 1 finely diced onion,
3 bruised cardamom pods, 2 teaspoons each of
ground cumin and ground coriander and ½ teaspoon
turmeric and cook over a low heat for 5–6 minutes
or until the onion is light golden. Add 1 deseeded
and chopped green chilli, 1 crushed garlic clove and
a thumb-sized piece of fresh root ginger, peeled
and grated, and cook for 1 minute, then add 425 g
(14 oz) prepared mixed vegetables, such as cauliflower,
peppers, carrots and courgettes, and cook for a further
5 minutes. Remove the pan from the heat and stir
through 200 ml (7 fl oz) yogurt and 2 tablespoons
ground almonds. Serve sprinkled with chopped
coriander. **Calories per serving 181**

monkfish kebabs

Calories per serving **211**
Serves **4**
Preparation time **10 minutes,
plus marinating**
Cooking time **8–10 minutes**

1 kg (2 lb) **monkfish fillet**, cut
into 4 cm (1½ inch) cubes
200 g (7 oz) **natural yogurt**
4 tablespoons **lemon juice**
3 **garlic cloves**, crushed
2 teaspoons grated **fresh root
ginger**
1 teaspoon **hot chilli powder**
1 teaspoon **ground cumin**
1 teaspoon **ground coriander**
2 **fresh red chillies**, finely
sliced
salt and **pepper**

To garnish
chopped **fresh coriander**
lime slices
sliced **fresh red chillies**

Put the monkfish cubes into a non-metallic bowl.

Mix together the yogurt, lemon juice, garlic, ginger, chilli powder, cumin, ground coriander and chillies in a small bowl, and season with salt and pepper. Pour this over the fish, cover and marinate in the refrigerator overnight, if time allows.

Lift the fish out of the marinade and thread on to 8 flat metal skewers. Place on a grill rack and cook under a preheated hot grill for 8–10 minutes, turning once, until the fish is cooked through. Serve hot, garnished with chopped fresh coriander, lime slices and chilli slices.

For tandoori whiting fillets, make a marinade using 200 g (7 oz) natural yogurt, 4 tablespoons lemon juice, 2 garlic cloves, crushed, 1 teaspoon grated fresh root ginger and 1 teaspoon ground coriander. Place 4 × 200 g (7 oz) whiting fillets in a non-metallic dish and pour over the marinade. Marinate the fish in the tandoori mixture overnight and cook as above. **Calories per serving 197**

spicy courgette fritters

Calories per serving **211**
Serves **4**
Preparation time **15 minutes,**
  plus draining
Cooking time **10–15 minutes**

3 **courgettes**
2 large **spring onions**, grated
1 **garlic clove**, finely chopped
finely grated rind of 1 **lemon**
4 tablespoons **gram flour**
2 teaspoons **medium curry**
  powder
1 **fresh red chilli**, deseeded
  and finely chopped
2 tablespoons finely chopped
  mint leaves
2 tablespoons finely chopped
  fresh coriander leaves
2 **eggs**, lightly beaten
2 tablespoons **light olive oil**
salt and **pepper**

Grate the courgettes into a colander. Sprinkle lightly with salt and leave for at least 1 hour to drain. Squeeze out the remaining liquid.

Place the remaining ingredients, except the eggs and olive oil, in a mixing bowl and add the courgettes. Season lightly, bearing in mind you have already salted the courgettes, and mix well. Add the eggs and mix again to combine.

Heat half the olive oil in a large frying pan over a medium-high heat. Place dessertspoonfuls of the mixture, well spaced, in the pan and press down with the back of the spoon. Cook for 1–2 minutes on each side, until golden and cooked through. Remove from the pan and keep warm. Repeat to cook the rest of the fritters in the same way, adding the remaining oil to the pan when necessary.

For cucumber, mango & fromage frais relish, to serve as an accompaniment, peel, deseed and coarsely grate 1 cucumber into a fine mesh sieve. Squeeze out any excess liquid using the back of a spoon. Place the grated cucumber in a bowl with 2 tablespoons hot mango chutney and 200 g (7 oz) fat-free fromage frais. Stir in a small handful of finely chopped coriander leaves, season and chill until required. **Calories per serving 60**

souffléd curried omelette

Calories per serving **212**
Serves **4**
Preparation time **25 minutes**
Cooking time **about 20
minutes**

1 tablespoon **groundnut oil**
4 **garlic cloves**, crushed
8 **spring onions**, finely sliced
1 **fresh red chilli**, finely sliced
1 tablespoon **medium curry
powder**
4 **tomatoes**, peeled,
deseeded and finely
chopped
small handful of finely chopped
fresh coriander leaves
small handful of finely chopped
mint leaves
8 large **eggs**, separated
salt and **pepper**

Heat half the oil in an ovenproof frying pan over a
medium heat. Add the garlic, spring onions and red
chilli and stir-fry for 1–2 minutes. Stir in the curry
powder, tomatoes and chopped herbs and stir-fry for
20–30 seconds. Remove from the heat, season to
taste and allow to cool slightly.

Place the egg whites in a large bowl and whisk until
soft peaks form. Gently beat the egg yolks in a separate
bowl, then fold into the egg whites with the tomato
mixture until well combined.

Wipe out the pan with kitchen paper and place over
a medium heat. Add the remaining oil and, when hot,
pour in the egg mixture. Reduce the heat and cook
gently for 8–10 minutes or until the base is starting to
set. Transfer the pan to a preheated medium-hot grill
and cook for 4–5 minutes or until the top is puffed,
lightly golden and almost set. Serve immediately with
a crisp green salad.

For Indian spicy scrambled eggs, heat 1 tablespoon
groundnut oil in a large nonstick frying pan over a gentle
heat. Beat 8 eggs in a bowl and add 1 finely chopped
red onion, 2 sliced green chillies, 1 finely chopped
tomato, 1 teaspoon grated peeled ginger and a small
handful of finely chopped coriander leaves. Season,
pour into the pan and cook, stirring occasionally, for
5–6 minutes or until lightly scrambled. **Calories per
serving 200**

74

crab malabar-hill

Calories per serving **214**
Serves **4**
Preparation time **10 minutes**
Cooking time **5–6 minutes**

2 tablespoons **vegetable oil**
3 **garlic cloves**, finely chopped
2 teaspoons finely chopped
   fresh root ginger
6 **spring onions**, very thinly
   sliced
3 **fresh red chillies**, deseeded
   and finely sliced
625 g (1 ¼ lb) **fresh white**
   crab meat
grated rind and juice of **1 lime**
4 tablespoons chopped **fresh**
   coriander
2 tablespoons chopped **mint**
   leaves
salt and **pepper**
crisp **lettuce leaves**, to serve

Heat the oil in a large wok or nonstick frying pan and add the garlic, ginger, spring onions and chillies. Fry, stirring constantly, for 2–3 minutes.

Add the crab meat, lime rind and juice, coriander and mint. Stir-fry for 2–3 minutes, season with salt and pepper and serve hot on top of crisp lettuce leaves.

For spicy crab omelettes, use this spicy, tangy crab mixture as the filling. Make 4 thin omelettes, using 2 eggs each, in a nonstick frying pan. Divide the crab mixture between them and fold over to enclose it. Serve with a crisp green salad. **Calories per serving 329**

thai red pork & bean curry

Calories per serving **216**
Serves **4**
Preparation time **10 minutes**
Cooking time **5 minutes**

2 tablespoons **groundnut oil**
1 ½ tablespoons **Thai red curry paste**
375 g (12 oz) **lean pork**, sliced into thin strips
100 g (3½ oz) **green beans**, trimmed and cut in half
2 tablespoons **Thai fish sauce**
1 teaspoon **caster sugar**
Chinese chives or **regular chives**, to garnish

Heat the oil in a wok or large frying pan over a medium heat until the oil starts to shimmer, add the curry paste and cook, stirring, until it releases its aroma.

Add the pork and beans and stir-fry for 2–3 minutes or until the meat is cooked through and the beans are just tender.

Stir in the fish sauce and sugar and serve, garnished with Chinese chives or regular chives.

For chicken green curry with sugar snap peas, replace the red curry paste with 1 ½ tablespoons green curry paste, the pork with 375 g (12 oz) sliced chicken breast and the green beans with 100 g (3½ oz) sliced sugar snap peas. Cook as above, adding a dash of lime juice before serving. **Calories per serving 204**

sri lankan scallop curry

Calories per serving **216**
Serves **4**
Preparation time **10 minutes**
Cooking time **20–25 minutes**

1 tablespoon **groundnut oil**
¼ teaspoon **turmeric**
1 teaspoon **cumin seeds**
2 **fresh red chillies**, deseeded
  and chopped
1 **onion**, finely chopped
6 **tomatoes**, peeled,
  deseeded and diced
3 tablespoons **medium curry
  powder**
1 tablespoon **coconut cream**
1 teaspoon **ground cumin**
1 teaspoon **garam masala**
400 g (13 oz) **fresh king
  scallops**
small handful of finely chopped
  fresh coriander leaves
salt and **pepper**

Heat the oil in a frying pan over a low heat. Add the turmeric, cumin seeds and chillies, and fry briefly to release the flavours. Add the onion and cook gently for 10 minutes until softened but not coloured.

Stir in the tomatoes and curry powder and simmer for 5 minutes or until the tomatoes have cooked down to a thick sauce. Stir in the coconut cream, ground cumin and garam masala and season to taste.

Add the scallops and cook for a few minutes until the scallops are just cooked through. Check the seasoning and adjust if necessary. Stir in the coriander and serve immediately.

For homemade garam masala, place 4 tablespoons coriander seeds, 2 tablespoons cumin seeds, 1 tablespoon black peppercorns, 1 tablespoon ground ginger, 1 teaspoon cardamom seeds, 4 cloves, 1 cinnamon stick and 1 crushed dried bay leaf in a frying pan. Dry-roast over a medium-low heat for a few minutes until fragrant. Remove from the heat and allow to cool. Tip the contents of the pan into a mini blender or clean electric coffee grinder, and grind to a fine powder. Store in an airtight container for up to 1 month, or in the refrigerator for up to 3 months. **Calories per tablespoon 2**

thai mussel curry with ginger

Calories per serving **217**
Serves **4**
Preparation time **30 minutes**
Cooking time **15 minutes**

½–1 **fresh red chilli**
2 **shallots**, quartered
1 **lemon grass stalk**
1 tablespoon peeled and finely
  chopped **fresh root ginger**
1 tablespoon **groundnut oil**
400 ml (14 fl oz) can **reduced-fat coconut milk**
4–5 **kaffir lime leaves**
150 ml (¼ pint) **fish stock**
2 teaspoons **Thai fish sauce**
1.5 kg (3 lb) **mussels**,
  scrubbed and debearded
small bunch of **fresh coriander**,
  torn into pieces, to garnish

Place the chilli, shallots, lemon grass and ginger into a mini blender and blend until finely chopped.

Heat the oil in large, deep saucepan, add the finely chopped ingredients and fry over a medium heat for 5 minutes, stirring until softened. Add the coconut milk, lime leaves, fish stock and fish sauce and cook for 3 minutes.

Add the mussels, cover the pan and cook for about 5 minutes or until the mussel shells have opened, discarding any that do not open. Spoon into warmed bowls and serve garnished with coriander.

For Thai chicken & aubergine curry, prepare the above recipe up to the end of the second step, replacing the fish stock with 250 ml (8 fl oz) chicken stock. Stir in 1 diced aubergine and 300 g (10 oz) chicken breast, cut into large chunks. Bring back to the boil, cover and simmer for 12–15 minutes, or until the chicken is cooked and the aubergine tender. Serve scattered with coriander. **Calories per serving 218**

singapore curried scallops

Calories per serving **225**
Serves **4**
Preparation time **10 minutes**
Cooking time **5 minutes**

24 fresh **king scallops**
3 tablespoons **mild curry
powder**
1 tablespoon **groundnut oil**
4 tablespoons **light soy sauce**
2 tablespoons **rice wine**
2 **fresh red chillies**, finely
sliced
7 cm (3 inch) piece of **fresh
root ginger**, peeled and
finely shredded
6 **spring onions**, finely sliced
salt and **pepper**

Place the scallops on a plate, dust the curry powder over them and lightly season to taste. Toss to mix well.

Heat the oil in a large nonstick frying pan. When it is very hot, add the scallops, spacing them out around the pan. Sear for 1–2 minutes on each side, then remove from the pan and arrange on a warmed serving platter.

Mix together the soy sauce and rice wine and sprinkle over the scallops. Scatter a little chilli, ginger and spring onion over each one, and serve immediately.

For mild scallop & coconut curry, heat 1 tablespoon groundnut oil in a large frying pan and add 1 finely chopped onion, 1 deseeded and finely chopped red chilli, 2 finely chopped garlic cloves and 1 teaspoon very finely diced ginger. Stir-fry for 3–4 minutes or until the onion has just softened, then add 1 tablespoon mild curry powder and stir-fry for 1 minute. Add 400 ml (14 fl oz) reduced-fat coconut milk and 200 ml (7 fl oz) tomato passata and bring to the boil. Reduce the heat to medium, and cook for 6–8 minutes, stirring often. Season to taste, stir in 24 fresh king scallops and cook for 4–5 minutes or until they are just cooked through. Remove from the heat and serve in warmed bowls. **Calories per serving 313**

indian-spiced pumpkin wedges

Calories per serving **292**
Serves **4**
Preparation time **15 minutes,
plus cooling**
Cooking time **15–20 minutes**

1 kg (2 lb) **pumpkin** or
butternut squash
1 teaspoon **cumin seeds**
1 teaspoon **coriander seeds**
2 **cardamom pods**
3 tablespoons **sunflower oil**
1 teaspoon **caster sugar** or
mango chutney

Coconut pesto
25 g (1 oz) **fresh coriander
leaves**
1 **garlic clove**, crushed
1 **fresh green chilli**, deseeded
and chopped
pinch of **caster sugar**
1 tablespoon **pistachio nuts**,
roughly chopped
6 tablespoons **coconut cream**
1 tablespoon **lime juice**
salt and **pepper**

Cut the pumpkin or butternut squash into thin wedges about 1 cm (½ inch) thick, discarding the seeds and fibres, and put in a large dish.

Heat a heavy-based frying pan until hot, add the whole spices and dry-fry over a medium heat, stirring, until browned. Leave to cool, then grind to a powder in a spice grinder or in a mortar with a pestle. Mix the ground spices with the oil and sugar or mango chutney in a small bowl, then add to the pumpkin wedges and toss well to coat.

Cook the pumpkin or squash wedges under a preheated hot grill, or over a preheated hot gas barbecue or the hot coals of a charcoal barbecue, for 6–8 minutes on each side until charred and tender.

Meanwhile, make the pesto. Put the coriander leaves, garlic, chilli, sugar and pistachio nuts in a food processor and process until fairly finely ground and blended. Season with salt and pepper. Add the coconut cream and lime juice and process again. Transfer to a serving bowl. Serve the wedges hot with the coconut pesto.

For Indian-spiced sweet potato wedges, cook 4 scrubbed sweet potatoes, 250 g (8 oz) each, in a large saucepan of simmering water for 15 minutes, or until just tender, then drain. When cool enough to handle, slice into large wedges. Toss with the spice and oil mixture and grill or barbecue, as above, for about 6 minutes, turning frequently, until browned. Serve hot with the coconut pesto. **Calories per serving 419**

creamy prawn curry

Calories per serving **248**
   (not including rice)
Serves **4**
Preparation time **10 minutes**
Cooking time **about**
10 minutes

2 tablespoons **vegetable oil**
1 **onion**, halved and finely
   sliced
2 **garlic cloves**, finely sliced
2.5 cm (1 inch) piece of **fresh**
   root ginger, peeled and
   finely chopped
1 tablespoon **ground**
   coriander
1 tablespoon **ground cumin**
½ teaspoon **turmeric**
200 ml (7 fl oz) **coconut milk**
125 ml (4 fl oz) **vegetable**
   stock
600 g (1 lb 3 oz) frozen large
   cooked **peeled prawns**,
   defrosted
grated rind and juice of 1 **lime**
4 tablespoons finely chopped
   fresh coriander leaves
salt and **pepper**

Heat the oil in a large saucepan, add the onion, garlic and ginger and cook for 4–5 minutes. Add the ground coriander, cumin and turmeric and cook, stirring, for 1 minute.

Pour in the coconut milk and stock and bring to the boil. Reduce the heat and simmer for 2–3 minutes. Stir in the prawns and lime rind and juice, then simmer for 2 minutes or until the prawns are heated through.

Stir in the chopped coriander and season well with salt and pepper. Serve immediately with boiled basmati or jasmine rice.

calcutta beef curry

Calories per serving **250**
Serves **4**
Preparation time **20 minutes,**
plus marinating
Cooking time **1 hour**
20 minutes

400 g (13 oz) **stewing beef,**
cut into bite-sized pieces
5 tablespoons **natural yogurt**
1 tablespoon **medium curry**
powder
2 tablespoons **mustard oil**
1 **dried bay leaf**
1 **cinnamon stick**
3 **cloves**
4 **green cardamom pods,**
bruised
1 **large onion,** halved and
thinly sliced
3 **garlic cloves,** crushed
1 teaspoon finely grated **fresh**
root ginger
1 teaspoon **ground turmeric**
1 teaspoon **hot chilli powder**
2 teaspoons **ground cumin**
400 ml (14 fl oz) **beef stock**
salt

Place the meat in a non-metallic bowl. Mix together
the yogurt and curry powder and pour over the meat.
Season with salt, cover and marinate in the refrigerator
for 24 hours.

Heat the oil in a large nonstick wok or frying pan and
add the spices. Stir-fry for 1 minute and then add the
onion. Stir-fry over a medium heat for 4–5 minutes, then
add the garlic, ginger, turmeric, chilli powder and cumin.
Add the marinated meat and stir-fry for 10–15 minutes
over a low heat.

Pour in the beef stock and bring to the boil. Reduce
the heat to low, cover tightly and simmer gently, stirring
occasionally, for 1 hour or until the meat is tender.
Check the seasoning, remove from the heat and
serve immediately.

For Calcutta chicken curry, use 4 chicken thighs
and 4 chicken drumsticks instead of the beef. Also
replace the beef stock with chicken stock. Follow the
same instructions as the recipe above. Add 100 g
(3½ oz) sliced ready-to-eat dried apricots for a hint of
sweetness, stirring them in with the stock. **Calories**
per serving 424

aubergine thai green curry

Calories per serving **262**
Serves **4**
Preparation time **7 minutes**
Cooking time **7–10 minutes**

300 ml (½ pint) **coconut milk**
40 g (1½ oz) **Thai green curry paste** (see page 208)
300 ml (½ pint) **vegetable stock**
4 **small round aubergines**, each cut into 8 pieces
40 g (1½ oz) **palm sugar**
1 teaspoon **salt**
4 teaspoons **vegetarian Thai fish sauce**
25 g (1 oz) **galangal** or **fresh root ginger**, peeled
425 g (14 oz) canned **straw mushrooms**, drained
50 g (2 oz) **green pepper**, thinly sliced

To garnish
handful of **Thai basil leaves**
2 tablespoons **coconut milk**

Heat the coconut milk in a saucepan with the curry paste, stirring to mix well. Add the stock and then the aubergines, sugar, salt, fish sauce, galangal or ginger and mushrooms.

Bring to the boil and cook, stirring, for 2 minutes.

Add the green pepper, lower the heat and cook for 1 minute. Serve in a bowl, garnished with the basil leaves and drizzled with coconut milk. Discard the piece of galangal or root ginger before serving.

For bamboo shoot & water chestnut curry, omit the aubergines and replace with 125 g (4 oz) canned bamboo shoots and 125 g (4 oz) canned sliced water chestnuts. Add at the same time as the mushrooms. Reduce the quantity of stock to 150 ml (¼ pint).
Calories per serving 255

thai squash, tofu & pea curry

Calories per serving **264**
Serves **4**
Preparation time **15 minutes**
Cooking time **25 minutes**

1 tablespoon **groundnut oil**
1 tablespoon **Thai red curry paste**
500 g (1 lb) peeled and deseeded **butternut squash,** cubed
450 ml (¾ pint) **vegetable stock**
400 ml (14 fl oz) can **reduced-fat coconut milk**
6 **kaffir lime leaves**, bruised, plus extra shredded leaves to garnish
200 g (7 oz) **fresh** or **frozen peas**
300 g (10 oz) **firm tofu**, diced
2 tablespoons **light soy** sauce
juice of 1 **lime**

To garnish
fresh coriander leaves
finely chopped **fresh red chilli**

Heat the oil in a wok or deep frying pan, add the curry paste and stir-fry over a low heat for 1 minute. Add the squash, stir-fry briefly and then add the stock, coconut milk and lime leaves.

Bring to the boil, then cover, reduce the heat and simmer gently for 15 minutes until the squash is tender.

Stir in the peas, tofu, soy sauce and lime juice and simmer for a further 5 minutes until the peas are cooked. Spoon into serving bowls and garnish with shredded lime leaves, chopped coriander and red chilli.

For Thai green vegetable curry, use green curry paste (see page 208 for homemade) instead of red curry paste. Replace the squash with 1 sliced carrot, 1 sliced courgette and 1 cored, deseeded and sliced red pepper and follow the recipe above. **Calories per serving 245**

lebanese tomato & courgette curry

Calories per serving **266**
Serves **4**
Preparation time **5 minutes**
Cooking time **40–45 minutes**

1 tablespoon **light olive oil**
1 large **onion**, finely chopped
4 **courgettes**, cut into
   1 × 3.5 cm (½ × 1½ inch)
   batons
2 × 400 g (13 oz) cans **whole
   plum tomatoes**
2 **garlic cloves**, crushed
½ teaspoon **chilli powder**
¼ teaspoon **ground turmeric**
2 teaspoons **dried mint**
salt and **pepper**
mint leaves, to garnish
150 g (5 oz) steamed **white
   rice** per person, to serve

Heat the oil in a large saucepan over a low heat. Add the onion and fry for 10–12 minutes until soft and translucent. Add the courgettes and cook for a further 5–6 minutes, stirring occasionally.

Add the tomatoes (including the juices) and garlic, and continue to cook over a medium heat for 20 minutes.

Stir in the chilli powder, turmeric and dried mint, and cook for a few more minutes to allow the flavours to mingle. Season to taste and serve with steamed white rice.

For spicy courgette & tomato bake, thickly slice 4 large courgettes and arrange in the base of a medium ovenproof dish. Mix a 400 g (13 oz) can chopped tomatoes with 6 tablespoons tomato purée, 100 ml (3½ fl oz) vegetable stock, 1 tablespoon hot curry powder, 2 teaspoons each of finely grated garlic and ginger, and 2 teaspoons dried mint. Season to taste and spoon over the courgettes. Cover with foil and cook in a preheated oven at 180°C (350°F), Gas Mark 4, for 25–30 minutes. Remove from the oven and serve with steamed rice. **Calories per serving 284**

spiced chicken & mango salad

Calories per serving **279**
Serves **4**
Preparation time **15 minutes**
Cooking time **5 minutes**

4 **boneless, skinless chicken breasts**, about 150 g (5 oz) each
6 teaspoons **mild curry paste**
4 tablespoons **lemon juice**
150 ml (¼ pint) **natural yogurt**
50 g (2 oz) **watercress**
½ **cucumber**, diced
½ **red onion**, finely chopped
1 **mango**, peeled, stoned and cut into chunks
½ **iceberg lettuce**

Cut the chicken breasts into long, thin slices. Put 4 teaspoons of the curry paste in a plastic bag with the lemon juice and mix together by squeezing the bag. Add the chicken and toss together.

Half-fill the base of a steamer with water and bring to the boil. Steam the chicken in a single layer, covered, for 5 minutes until cooked. Test with a knife or metal skewer; the juices will run clear when it is done.

Meanwhile, mix the remaining curry paste in a bowl with the yogurt.

Tear the watercress into bite-sized pieces. Add it to the yogurt dressing with the cucumber, red onion and mango and toss gently.

Tear the lettuce into pieces and arrange on 4 plates. Spoon the mango mixture over the top, add the warm chicken strips and serve immediately.

For chilli prawn, mango & avocado salad, replace the chicken with 400 g (13 oz) peeled, raw tiger prawns with the tails on. Prepare the salad in the same way as above but add the diced flesh of an avocado. Heat 2 tablespoons vegetable or groundnut oil in a nonstick frying pan over a high heat, and fry 1 finely chopped red chilli for 1 minute, then add the prawns and 2 finely chopped garlic cloves. Fry for 2 minutes until the prawns are pink and just cooked through. Mix through the salad and serve immediately. **Calories per serving 343**

spiced chickpeas with kale

Calories per serving **286**
Serves **4**
Preparation time **10 minutes**
Cooking time **35 minutes**

3 tablespoons **vegetable oil**
3 **red onions**, cut into wedges
2 tablespoons **mild curry paste**
400 g (13 oz) can **chopped tomatoes**
400 g (13 oz) can **chickpeas**, drained
300 ml (½ pint) **vegetable stock**
2 teaspoons **soft light brown sugar**
100 g (3½ oz) **curly kale**, chopped
salt and **pepper**

Heat the oil in a large saucepan and fry the onions for 5 minutes until beginning to colour. Stir in the curry paste and then the tomatoes, chickpeas, stock and sugar.

Bring to the boil, then reduce the heat, cover and simmer gently for 20 minutes.

Stir in the kale and cook gently for a further 10 minutes. Season to taste with salt and pepper and serve.

For sesame flatbreads, to serve as an accompaniment, place 250 g (8 oz) plain flour, 1 teaspoon salt and 25 g (1 oz) sesame seeds in a bowl. Add 3 tablespoons vegetable oil and 125 ml (4 fl oz) cold water and mix with a round-bladed knife to a dough, adding a dash more water if the dough feels dry. Divide into 8 pieces and very thinly roll out each piece on a lightly floured surface until about 2.5 mm (⅛ inch) thick. Heat a griddle or large dry frying pan until hot and cook the flatbreads for about 2 minutes on each side until pale golden. Serve one warm flatbread per person, and freeze the remainder. **Calories per serving 167**

baby aubergines with chilli

Calories per serving **297**
Serves **4**
Preparation time **20 minutes**
Cooking time **25–30 minutes**

500 g (1 lb) **baby aubergines**
5 tablespoons **sunflower oil**
6 **garlic cloves**, finely chopped
1 tablespoon finely chopped
  fresh root ginger
8 **spring onions**, cut
  diagonally into 2.5 cm
  (1 inch) lengths
2 **fresh red chillies**, deseeded
  and finely sliced
3 tablespoons **light soy sauce**
1 tablespoon **Chinese rice
  wine**
1 tablespoon **palm sugar**
small handful of **mint leaves**
small handful of roughly
  chopped **fresh coriander**
100 g (3½ oz) canned **water
  chestnuts**, roughly chopped
50 g (2 oz) **roasted peanuts**,
  roughly chopped

Cut the aubergines in half lengthways and place on a heatproof plate. Place a trivet or steamer rack in a wok and pour in about 5 cm (2 inches) of water. Bring the water to the boil and lower the aubergine plate on to the trivet or rack.

Reduce the heat, cover and steam for 25–30 minutes (replenishing the water in the wok if needed) until the aubergines are cooked through and soft to the touch. Remove the aubergines from the wok, transfer to a serving platter and allow to cool.

Meanwhile, heat the oil in a nonstick frying pan. Add the garlic, ginger, spring onions and chillies and stir-fry for 2–3 minutes. Remove from the heat and stir in the soy sauce, rice wine and sugar.

Toss the mint leaves, coriander and water chestnuts with the aubergines and pour the garlic and ginger mixture evenly over the top. Sprinkle over the peanuts, toss gently and serve immediately with lime wedges and steamed egg noodles or rice, if liked.

For aubergine with bamboo shoots, use 2 large aubergines instead of the baby one. Chop them into large dice and proceed as above. Add 50 g (2 oz) fresh red radishes, thinly sliced, and 100 g (3½ oz) canned bamboo shoots, drained, instead of water chestnuts. **Calories per serving 297**

spicy crab curry

Calories per serving **299**
Serves **4**
Preparation time **15 minutes**
Cooking time **40 minutes**

2 **cooked fresh crabs**, about
  750 g (1 ½ lb) each
3 **onions**, finely chopped
6 **garlic cloves**, finely chopped
1 tablespoon peeled and finely
  grated **fresh root ginger**
½ teaspoon **fenugreek seeds**
10 **curry leaves**
1 **cinnamon stick**
2 teaspoons **chilli powder**
1 teaspoon **ground turmeric**
400 ml (14 fl oz) can
  reduced-fat coconut milk
salt and **pepper**

Divide each crab into portions, by first removing the main shell. Next remove the two large claws and use a sharp knife to cut the body into 2 pieces, leaving the legs attached.

Place the onions, garlic, ginger, fenugreek, curry leaves, cinnamon, chilli, turmeric and coconut milk in a large saucepan. Season to taste, then cover and simmer gently for 30 minutes.

Add the crabs to the simmering sauce and cook for 10 minutes to heat through. Serve immediately, with plenty of napkins.

For spicy crab with angel hair pasta, cook 350 g (11 ½ oz) angel hair pasta according to packet instructions. Meanwhile, heat 1 tablespoon groundnut oil in a large frying pan over a gentle heat and add 3 finely chopped garlic cloves, 1 finely chopped red chilli, 6 finely chopped spring onions, 6 tablespoons reduced-fat coconut milk and 400 g (13 oz) white crab meat. Season and stir-fry for 3–4 minutes. Drain the pasta and add to the crab mixture. Toss to mix well and serve immediately. **Calories per serving 488**

malaysian coconut vegetables

Calories per serving **251**
Serves **4**
Preparation time **15 minutes,
plus soaking**
Cooking time **20 minutes**

125 g (4 oz) **broccoli florets**
125 g (4 oz) **French beans**,
cut into 2.5 cm (1 inch)
lengths
1 **red pepper**, cored,
deseeded and sliced
125 g (4 oz) **courgettes**,
thinly sliced

Coconut sauce
25 g (1 oz) **tamarind pulp**
150 ml (¼ pint) boiling **water**
400 ml (14 fl oz) can **coconut
milk**
2 teaspoons **Thai green curry
paste** (see page 208)
1.25 cm (½ inch) piece of
fresh root ginger, peeled
and finely grated
1 **onion**, cut into small cubes
½ teaspoon **ground turmeric**
salt

Make the coconut sauce. Put the tamarind in a bowl.
Pour over the measurement water and leave to soak
for 30 minutes. Mash the tamarind in the water, then
push through a sieve set over another bowl, squashing
the tamarind so that you get as much of the pulp as
possible; discard the stringy bits and any seeds.

Take 2 tablespoons of the cream from the top of the
coconut milk and pour it into a wok or large frying pan.
Add the curry paste, ginger, onion and turmeric, and
cook over a gentle heat, stirring, for 2–3 minutes. Stir
in the rest of the coconut milk and the tamarind water.
Bring to the boil, then reduce the heat to a simmer and
add a pinch of salt.

Add the broccoli to the coconut sauce and cook for
5 minutes, then add the green beans and red pepper.
Cook, stirring, for another 5 minutes. Finally, stir in the
courgettes and cook gently for 1–2 minutes until the
courgette is just tender. Serve immediately with some
crispy prawn crackers, if liked.

For chicken & green beans in coconut sauce,
soak the tamarind and make the coconut sauce as
above. Add 500 g (1 lb) diced boneless, skinless
chicken breast to the wok or frying pan. Simmer for
5 minutes, then add the sliced French beans, omitting
the red pepper and courgettes. Simmer gently for
another 5 minutes until the chicken is cooked through.
Calories per serving 365

recipes under 400 calories

chicken kofta curry

Calories per serving **343**
Serves **4**
Preparation time **15 minutes**
Cooking time **25 minutes**

750 g (1½ lb) **minced chicken**
2 teaspoons peeled and finely grated **fresh root ginger**
2 **garlic cloves**, crushed
2 teaspoons **fennel seeds**, crushed
1 teaspoon **ground cinnamon**
1 teaspoon **chilli powder**
cooking oil spray
500 ml (17 fl oz) **tomato passata with onions and garlic**
1 teaspoon **ground turmeric**
2 tablespoons **medium curry powder**
1 teaspoon **agave syrup**
salt and **pepper**

To serve
100 ml (3½ fl oz) **fat-free natural yogurt**, whisked
pinch of **chilli powder**
chopped **mint leaves**

Place the mince in a bowl with the ginger, garlic, fennel seeds, cinnamon and chilli powder. Season to taste and mix thoroughly with your hands until well combined. Form the mixture into walnut-sized balls.

Spray a large nonstick frying pan with cooking oil spray and place over a medium heat. Add the chicken balls and stir-fry for 4–5 minutes or until lightly browned. Transfer to a plate and keep warm.

Pour the passata into the frying pan and add the turmeric, curry powder and agave syrup. Bring to the boil, then reduce the heat to a simmer, season to taste and carefully place the chicken balls in the sauce. Cover and cook gently for 15–20 minutes, turning the balls occasionally, until they are cooked through.

Serve immediately, drizzled with the yogurt and sprinkled with chilli powder and mint leaves.

For quick chunky chicken Madras, replace the minced chicken with cubed, boneless, skinless chicken breasts and the medium curry powder with Madras curry powder. Cook as above and add 300 g (10 oz) peas for the last 5 minutes of cooking. Serve hot. **Calories per serving 387**

spiced pumpkin & spinach soup

Calories per serving **302**
Serves **4**
Preparation time **10 minutes**
Cooking time **30–32 minutes**

50 g (2 oz) **butter**
2 tablespoons **olive oil**
1 **onion**, roughly chopped
2 **garlic cloves**, peeled
1.5 kg (3 lb) **pumpkin**, peeled
  and roughly chopped
1 teaspoon **ground coriander**
½ teaspoon **cayenne pepper**
½ teaspoon **ground
  cinnamon**
¼ teaspoon **ground allspice**
750 ml (1¼ pints) **hot
  vegetable stock**
150 g (5 oz) **frozen spinach**
salt and **pepper**

To serve
2 tablespoons **pumpkin
  seeds**, lightly toasted
4 teaspoons **pumpkin
  seed oil**

Heat the butter and oil in a large, heatproof casserole
and add the onion and garlic. Cook over a medium heat
for 5–6 minutes until soft and golden.

Add the pumpkin and continue cooking for a further
8 minutes, stirring frequently, until beginning to soften
and turn golden. Add the spices and cook for 2–3 minutes,
making sure that the pumpkin is well coated.

Pour in the hot stock and bring to the boil, then reduce
the heat, cover and leave to bubble gently for about
15 minutes until the pumpkin is soft.

Use a hand-held blender to liquidize the pumpkin
until smooth, then stir in the spinach. Reheat for about
5 minutes until the spinach has melted and the soup
is hot. Season to taste.

Spoon the soup into bowls, scatter over the lightly
toasted pumpkin seeds and a drizzle of pumpkin seed
oil and serve immediately.

For butternut, spinach & coconut soup, use 500 g
(1 lb) butternut squash, peeled, deseeded and cubed,
instead of the pumpkin, and cook as above. Stir in 200 ml
(7 fl oz) reduced-fat coconut milk before serving.
Calories per serving 357

curried crab & prawn cakes

Calories per serving **305**
Serves **4**
Preparation time **10 minutes,
   plus chilling**
Cooking time **20–25 minutes**

400 g (13 oz) **fresh white
   crabmeat**
400 g (13 oz) **raw tiger
   prawns**, peeled and
   deveined
1 tablespoon **hot curry
   powder**
2 **garlic cloves**, crushed
1 teaspoon peeled and grated
   fresh root ginger
1 **fresh red chilli**, deseeded
   and finely chopped
4 tablespoons finely chopped
   red onion
8 tablespoons chopped **fresh
   coriander leaves**, plus extra
   to garnish
1 **small egg**, beaten
100 g (3½ oz) **fresh
   wholemeal breadcrumbs**
cooking oil spray
salt and **pepper**
lemon wedges, to serve

Place the crabmeat, prawns, curry powder, garlic, ginger, chilli, onion, coriander, egg and breadcrumbs in a food processor. Season well and pulse for a few seconds until well mixed. Transfer to a bowl, cover and chill in the refrigerator for 5–6 hours or overnight.

Preheat the oven to 200°C (400°F), Gas Mark 6, line a baking sheet with greaseproof paper and spray with a little cooking oil spray.

Divide the crab mixture into 16 equal portions and shape each into a round cake. Arrange on the prepared baking sheet, spray with a little cooking oil spray and bake for 20–25 minutes until lightly browned and cooked through. Garnish with coriander and serve immediately with lemon wedges.

For piquant crab, prawn & rice salad, place 400g (13 oz) each of fresh white crabmeat and cooked peeled prawns in a salad bowl with 250 g (8 oz) cold cooked basmati rice. Add 6 finely sliced spring onions, ½ finely diced cucumber, 10 halved cherry tomatoes and a small handful of chopped coriander leaves. In a small bowl, whisk 3 tablespoons light olive oil with 4 tablespoons lemon juice, 1 teaspoon agave syrup and 1 finely chopped red chilli. Season, pour over the salad and toss to mix well. **Calories per serving 383**

thai red chicken curry

Calories per serving **307**
Serves **4**
Preparation time **15 minutes**
Cooking time **35 minutes**

1 tablespoon **sunflower oil**
3 **shallots**, finely chopped
3 **garlic cloves**, finely chopped
2 tablespoons **Thai red curry paste**
2 teaspoons **galangal paste**
400 ml (14 fl oz) can **reduced-fat coconut milk**
2 teaspoons **Thai fish sauce**
1 teaspoon **palm sugar** or **soft light brown sugar**
3 **kaffir lime leaves**
6 boneless, skinless **chicken thighs**, diced
handful of **Thai basil leaves** (optional)

Heat the oil in a saucepan over a medium heat, add the shallots and garlic and fry for 3–4 minutes until softened. Stir in the curry paste and galangal paste and cook for 1 minute. Mix in the coconut milk, fish sauce, sugar and lime leaves and bring to the boil.

Stir in the chicken, then reduce the heat, cover and simmer for 30 minutes, or until the chicken is cooked through, stirring occasionally. Stir in the basil leaves, if using, and serve.

For Thai green chicken curry, make the curry as above, adding 2 peeled and finely chopped lemon grass stalks when frying the shallots and garlic. Replace the red curry paste with 2 tablespoons Thai green curry paste (see page 208 for homemade) and stir in, then continue as above. To finish, stir in the grated rind of 1 lime and lime juice to taste, garnish with chopped coriander and serve immediately. **Calories per serving 318**

tandoori chicken

Calories per serving **319**
Serves **4**
Preparation time **5 minutes,
  plus marinating**
Cooking time **25–30 minutes**

4 **chicken drumsticks**
4 **chicken thighs**
2 tablespoons **tikka spice mix**
  or **paste**
2 **garlic cloves**, crushed
1 tablespoon **tomato purée**
juice of 1 **lemon**
75 ml (3 fl oz) **natural yogurt**

To garnish
grated **lime** rind
chopped **coriander**

Make deep slashes all over the chicken pieces. In a large glass or ceramic bowl, mix all the remaining ingredients, then add the chicken and turn to coat thoroughly with the marinade. Cover and leave to marinate in the refrigerator for at least 30 minutes or overnight.

Transfer the chicken to an ovenproof dish and cook in a preheated oven, 240°C (475°F), Gas Mark 9, for 25–30 minutes until cooked through, tender and lightly charred at the edges. Serve garnished with lime rind and chopped coriander.

For blackened tandoori salmon, use the marinade above to coat 4 thick, skinless salmon fillets, about 175 g (6 oz) each, then cover and leave to marinate in the refrigerator for 30 minutes–1 hour. Transfer to a nonstick baking sheet and bake at 180°C (350°F), Gas Mark 4, for 20 minutes or until cooked through. **Calories per serving 377**

cambodian fish curry

Calories per serving **323**
Serves **4**
Preparation time **10 minutes**
Cooking time **15 minutes**

2 tablespoons finely chopped
  lemon grass (tough outer
  leaves removed)
1 tablespoon peeled and finely
  chopped **galangal**
3 **fresh red chillies**, roughly
  chopped
4 **garlic cloves**, roughly
  chopped
200 ml (7 fl oz) **water**
750 g (1½ lb) thick **halibut
  fillet**, skinned and cubed
1 tablespoon **groundnut oil**
200 ml (7 fl oz) **reduced-fat
  coconut milk**
1 tablespoon **Thai fish sauce**
2 tablespoons chopped
  dry-roasted peanuts
small handful of **Thai basil
  leaves**

Place the lemon grass, galangal, chillies and garlic
in a mini blender with the measured water and blend
to a smooth paste. Set aside.

Pat the fish dry with kitchen paper, arrange on a
grill rack and cook under a medium-hot grill for
10–12 minutes or until cooked through.

Meanwhile, heat the oil in a nonstick frying pan and
stir-fry the spice paste for 4–5 minutes. Add the
coconut milk and fish sauce and cook, stirring, over
a high heat for 5 minutes. Add the fish to the pan
with the peanuts and basil, and toss gently to mix well.
Serve immediately.

For spicy fish with lemon grass & coconut, place
4 thick cod fillets in a shallow, lightly greased ovenproof
dish in a single layer. Mix together 2 tablespoons finely
chopped lemon grass, 2 finely chopped fresh red chillies,
2 teaspoons each of grated fresh root ginger and garlic
and 100 ml (3½ fl oz) reduced-fat coconut milk. Season
and spoon over the fish. Cook in a preheated oven at
180°C (350°F), Gas Mark 4, for 15–20 minutes or
until cooked through. Serve garnished with chopped
coriander. **Calories per serving 182**

spicy marinated lamb chops

Calories per serving **346**
Serves **4**
Preparation time **10 minutes,
plus marinating**
Cooking time **8–10 minutes**

12 small **lamb chops**, trimmed
125 ml (4 fl oz) **fat-free
natural yogurt**
4 tablespoons **tomato purée**
4 tablespoons **medium curry
paste**
1 teaspoon grated **garlic**
1 teaspoon peeled and finely
grated **fresh root ginger**
large pinch of **sea salt**
3 tablespoons **lemon juice**

To serve
1 **red onion**, sliced
4 **tomatoes**, sliced
½ **cucumber**, sliced

Arrange the chops in a single layer in a shallow non-metallic dish. Mix the yogurt with the tomato purée, curry paste, garlic, ginger, sea salt and lemon juice, and rub into the lamb. Cover and marinate in the refrigerator for 4–5 hours or overnight.

Preheat the oven to 220°C (425°F), Gas Mark 7, and line a large roasting tin with foil. Arrange the chops in a single layer in the tin and cook in the preheated oven for 8–10 minutes, turning halfway through cooking, or until the lamb is cooked to your liking. Serve immediately with onion rings and tomato and cucumber slices.

For spicy beef skewers, cut 750 g (1 ½ lb) lean beef fillet into large cubes and place in a non-metallic dish. Mix together the marinade as above and pour over the beef. Toss to mix well and marinate in the refrigerator for 6–8 hours or overnight. When ready to cook, thread the marinated beef on to 8 metal skewers and grill under a medium-hot grill for 3–4 minutes on each side or until cooked to your liking. Serve with onion rings and tomato and cucumber slices. **Calories per serving 431**

indonesian yellow drumstick curry

Calories per serving **383**
Serves **4**
Preparation time **15 minutes**
Cooking time **40–45 minutes**

2 **fresh red chillies**, roughly
  chopped, plus extra to garnish
2 **shallots**, roughly chopped
3 **garlic cloves**, chopped
4 tablespoons chopped **lemon
  grass** (outer leaves removed)
1 tablespoon peeled and finely
  chopped **galangal**
2 teaspoons **ground turmeric**
1 teaspoon **cayenne pepper**
1 teaspoon **ground coriander**
1 teaspoon **ground cumin**
¼ teaspoon **ground cinnamon**
3 tablespoons **Thai fish sauce**
1 tablespoon **palm sugar** or
  brown sugar
4 **kaffir lime leaves**, shredded
400 ml (14 fl oz) can **reduced-
  fat coconut milk**
juice of ½ **lime**
8 large **chicken drumsticks**,
  skinned
200 g (7 oz) **baby new
  potatoes**, peeled
10–12 **Thai basil leaves**,
  to garnish

Place the chillies, shallots, garlic, lemon grass, galangal,
turmeric, cayenne, coriander, cumin, cinnamon, fish
sauce, sugar, lime leaves, coconut milk and lime juice
in a food processor, and blend until fairly smooth.

Arrange the chicken drumsticks in a single layer in
an ovenproof casserole. Scatter over the potatoes.
Pour over the spice paste to coat the chicken and
potatoes evenly. Cover and cook in a preheated oven,
for 40–45 minutes until the chicken is cooked through
and the potatoes are tender. Serve hot, garnished with
basil and chopped red chilli.

For tandoori drumstick curry, arrange 8 large,
skinned chicken drumsticks in a single layer in an
ovenproof casserole. Mix 300 ml (½ pint) fat-free
natural yogurt with 4 tablespoons tandoori paste and
the juice of 2 lemons. Season and pour this mixture
over the chicken to coat evenly. Cover and cook in
a preheated oven at 180°C (350°), Gas Mark 4, for
35–40 minutes, then uncover and continue to cook for
10–15 minutes or until cooked through. Serve warm
with a crisp green salad. **Calories per serving 360**

spinach & chicken curry

Calories per serving **351**

Serves **4**

Preparation time **15 minutes, plus marinating**

Cooking time **1 hour**

5 tablespoons **natural yogurt**

2 tablespoons crushed **garlic**

2 tablespoons grated **fresh root ginger**

1 tablespoon **ground coriander**

1 tablespoon **mild curry powder**

750 g (1½ lb) **boneless, skinless chicken thighs**, cut into bite-sized pieces

400 g (13 oz) **frozen whole-leaf spinach**, thawed

2 tablespoons **sunflower oil**

1 **onion**, finely chopped

2 teaspoons **cumin seeds**

100 ml (3½ fl oz) **water**

1 tablespoon **lemon juice**

salt and **pepper**

Mix together the yogurt, garlic, ginger, ground coriander and curry powder. Season well. Place the chicken in a large, non-metallic bowl and pour over the yogurt mixture. Toss to mix well, cover and marinate in the refrigerator for 8–10 hours.

Place the spinach in a saucepan and cook over a medium heat for 6–8 minutes. Season and drain thoroughly. Place the cooked spinach in a food processor and blend until smooth.

Heat the oil in a large nonstick frying pan and add the onion. Cook over a gentle heat for 10–12 minutes, then add the cumin seeds and stir-fry for 1 minute. Increase the heat to high, add the chicken mixture and stir-fry for 6–8 minutes. Pour in the measured water and the spinach and bring to the boil.

Reduce the heat to low, cover tightly and cook for 25–30 minutes or until the chicken is cooked through.

Uncover the pan, check the seasoning and cook over a high heat for 3–4 minutes, stirring constantly. Remove from the heat and stir in the lemon juice. Serve immediately.

For cauliflower & chicken curry, substitute ½ a cauliflower for the spinach. Cut the cauliflower into small florets, and halve the larger florets. Proceed as above, adding the cauliflower to the curry when you add the water. **Calories per serving 346**

spiced mussel curry

Calories per serving **353**
Serves **4**
Preparation time **10 minutes**
Cooking time **10–12 minutes**

1 kg (2 lb) **live mussels**
1 tablespoon **vegetable oil**
1 **onion**, finely chopped
4 **garlic cloves**, crushed
3 **green chillies**, finely
  chopped
1 teaspoon **ground turmeric**
100 ml (3½ fl oz) **white wine
  vinegar**
400 ml (14 fl oz) can **coconut
  milk**
2 teaspoons **sugar**
4 tablespoons chopped **fresh
  coriander**
salt and **pepper**
grated fresh coconut, to
  garnish

Rinse the mussels under cold running water and scrape off any beards. Discard any that are open or that do not close when sharply tapped. Drain and set aside.

Heat the oil in a large saucepan, add the onion, garlic, chillies and turmeric and fry for 2–3 minutes. Add the mussels, vinegar, coconut milk, sugar and coriander. Stir well and bring to the boil.

Cover and cook gently for 5–6 minutes or until all the mussels have opened. Discard any that remain shut.

Transfer the mussels to a serving bowl with a slotted spoon, season the cooking juices and pour over the mussels. Garnish with grated coconut and serve.

For sweet & sour mussel curry, add half a pineapple, woody sections of core removed and the flesh cut into bite-sized chunks. Add to the curry at the same time as the mussels and proceed as above. **Calories per serving 369**

balti chicken

Calories per serving **388**
Serves **4**
Preparation time **15 minutes**
Cooking time **20–25 minutes**

1 tablespoon **groundnut oil**
2 **onions**, thinly sliced
2 **fresh red chillies**, deseeded
  and thinly sliced
6–8 **curry leaves**
200 ml (7 fl oz) **water**
3 **garlic cloves**, crushed
1 teaspoon peeled and finely
  grated **fresh root ginger**
1 tablespoon **ground**
  coriander
2 tablespoons **Madras curry**
  powder
500 g (1 lb) **minced chicken**
400 g (13 oz) **fresh** or **frozen**
  peas
4 tablespoons **lemon juice**
small handful of chopped
  mint leaves
small handful of chopped **fresh**
  coriander
salt

To serve
chapatis (1 per person)
fat-free natural yogurt
  (2 tablespoons per serving)

Heat the oil in a large wok or frying pan over a medium heat. Add the onion, chilli and curry leaves, and stir-fry for 4–5 minutes. Add 4 tablespoons of the measured water and continue to stir-fry for a further 2–3 minutes.

Add the garlic, ginger, ground coriander, curry powder and chicken, and stir-fry over a high heat for 10 minutes. Add the remaining measured water and the peas, and continue to cook for 6–8 minutes until the chicken is cooked through.

Remove from the heat and stir in the lemon juice and herbs. Season to taste, and serve immediately with warmed chapatis and yogurt.

For creamy chicken & vegetable curry, heat 1 tablespoon groundnut oil in a large wok or frying pan. Add 1 chopped onion, 1 sliced red chilli, 6 curry leaves, 2 teaspoons each of crushed fresh root ginger and garlic, and 2 tablespoons mild curry powder. Stir-fry for 1–2 minutes, then add 625 g (1 ¼ lb) diced boneless, skinless chicken breasts. Stir-fry for 3–4 minutes, then add 500 ml (17 fl oz) chicken stock and 200 ml (7 fl oz) reduced-fat coconut milk. Bring to the boil and cook for 12–15 minutes or until the chicken is cooked through. Stir in 200 g (7 oz) frozen peas and cook over a high heat for 4–5 minutes. Season and serve with rice (approximately 3 tablespoons per person). **Calories per serving 470**

creamy tandoori chicken kebabs

Calories per serving **356**
Serves **4**
Preparation time **15 minutes,
plus marinating**
Cooking time **6–8 minutes**

750 g (1½ lb) **boneless,
skinless chicken thighs,**
cut into bite-sized pieces
150 g (5 oz) **natural yogurt,**
lightly whisked
100 ml (3½ fl oz) **single cream**
2 teaspoons **crushed garlic**
2 teaspoons grated **fresh root
ginger**
2 tablespoons **medium curry
powder**
4 tablespoons **garam masala**
(see page 80)
1 teaspoon **ground
cardamom seeds**
2 tablespoons **tomato purée**
4 tablespoons **lemon juice**
1 tablespoon **tandoori spice
powder**
sunflower oil, for brushing
2 **limes,** halved

Red onion salad
4 **red onions**
salt and **pepper**
juice of 2 **lemons**

Place the chicken in a large, non-metallic dish. To make
the marinade, mix together all the remaining ingredients,
season well and pour over the chicken. Cover and chill
for 24–48 hours.

When ready to cook, allow the chicken to come to
room temperature.

Meanwhile slice the onions into thin rings and place in
a large mixing bowl. Season with salt and pepper and
squeeze over the juice of the lemons. Cover and allow
to stand for 30 minutes before tossing and serving with
the kebabs.

Divide the chicken pieces between 8–12 metal
skewers, place on a lightly oiled grill rack in a single
layer and lightly brush with sunflower oil.

Place the kebabs under a medium-hot grill and cook
for 3–4 minutes on each side, or until cooked through.
Alternatively, cook in a preheated oven at 200°C
(400°F), Gas Mark 6 for 8–10 minutes. Serve with the
red onion salad and lime halves for squeezing over.

For spicy Sunday roast, try marinating a whole
chicken in this creamy marinade. Cover and chill for
24–48 hours, then bring back to room temperature
before roasting it in a preheated oven at 200°C (400°F),
Gas Mark 6 for 1¼ hours or until the chicken is cooked
through. **Calories per serving 358**

stuffed aubergines with lamb

Calories per serving **361**
Serves **4**
Preparation time **20 minutes**
Cooking time **45 minutes**

2 large **aubergines**
1 tablespoon **groundnut oil**
1 **onion**, thinly sliced
1 teaspoon peeled and finely
grated **fresh root ginger**
1 teaspoon **hot chilli powder**
1 tablespoon **medium curry
paste**
2 **garlic cloves**, crushed
¼ teaspoon **ground turmeric**
1 teaspoon **ground coriander**
2 teaspoons **dried mint**
1 **ripe tomato**, finely chopped
500 g (1 lb) lean **minced
lamb**
100 g (3½ oz) **roasted red
peppers** in brine, drained
and finely diced
2 tablespoons chopped **fresh
coriander leaves**
2 tablespoons chopped **mint
leaves**
salt

Preheat the oven to 180°C (350°F), Gas Mark 4.
Cut the aubergines in half lengthways, use a spoon to
scoop out most of the flesh and discard it. Place the
aubergines, cut sides up, on a baking sheet and set aside.

Heat the oil in a large frying pan over a medium heat.
Add the onion and stir-fry for 4–5 minutes until soft.
Now add the ginger, chilli powder, curry paste, garlic,
turmeric, ground coriander, dried mint and chopped
tomato, and stir-fry for 4–5 minutes. Season to taste.

Add the lamb and continue to stir-fry for 5–6 minutes
over a high heat until well browned. Stir in the red
pepper and herbs and mix well. Spoon the lamb mixture
into the prepared aubergine shells and cook in the
preheated oven for 20–25 minutes. Serve immediately.

For minced lamb & aubergine curry, heat 1 tablespoon
groundnut oil in a nonstick wok or frying pan and add
1 finely chopped onion, 2 crushed garlic cloves,
2 teaspoons grated fresh root ginger and 2 sliced fresh
red chillies, and stir-fry for 3–4 minutes. Cut 1 large
aubergine into 1.5 cm (¾ inch) cubes, add to the pan
and stir-fry for 2–3 minutes. Add 2 tablespoons medium
curry powder and 625 g (1¼ lb) extra-lean minced
lamb and stir-fry for 6–8 minutes over a high heat until
sealed. Stir in a 400 g (13 oz) can chopped tomatoes
and 1 teaspoon agave syrup and season to taste. Cook
over a medium heat for 6–8 minutes or until the lamb is
tender and cooked through. Remove from the heat, add
a handful each of chopped coriander and mint leaves,
and serve. **Calories per serving 371**

pork & lemon grass curry

Calories per serving **362**
Serves **4**
Preparation time **20 minutes**
Cooking time **40 minutes**

4 tablespoons **sunflower oil**
750 g (1½ lb) **minced pork**
8 tablespoons finely **chopped lemon grass**
3 **garlic cloves**, crushed
2 teaspoons **grated galangal** or **fresh root ginger**
1 tablespoon **Thai green curry paste** (see page 208)
1 teaspoon **ground turmeric**
2 **fresh green chillies**, chopped
150 ml (¼ pint) **water**
400 ml (14 fl oz) can **coconut milk**
4 **lime leaves**, finely shredded
200 g (7 oz) **sugarsnap peas**, trimmed
2 tablespoons **lime juice**
salt and **pepper**

Heat half the oil in a large, nonstick wok and brown the pork over a high heat for 3–4 minutes. Remove from the wok and set aside.

Place the lemon grass, garlic, galangal or ginger, curry paste, turmeric and chillies in a food processor with the measured water and process until smooth.

Add the remaining oil to the wok and place over a high heat. Add the lemon grass paste and stir-fry for 2–3 minutes, then add the pork and stir-fry for a further 2–3 minutes.

Stir in the coconut milk and lime leaves, season and bring to the boil. Reduce the heat and simmer, uncovered, for 30 minutes, stirring occasionally.

Add the sugarsnap peas 6 minutes before the end of cooking and stir to mix well.

Remove from the heat and stir in the lime juice before serving.

For pork & vegetable lemon grass curry, use 150 g (5 oz) each of fine green beans and carrots. Cut the carrots into short thin batons. Cook as above, omitting the sugarsnap peas. **Calories per serving 372**

salmon in banana leaves

Calories per serving **366**
Serves **4**
Preparation time **15 minutes**
Cooking time **15 minutes**

large bunch of **fresh
    coriander**, roughly chopped
3 tablespoons chopped
mint leaves
2 **garlic cloves**, crushed
1 teaspoon grated **fresh root
    ginger**
4 **fresh red chillies**, deseeded
    and chopped
2 teaspoons **ground cumin**
1 teaspoon **ground coriander**
2 teaspoons **soft brown
    sugar**
2 tablespoons **lime juice**
150 ml (¼ pint) **coconut milk**
4 **thick salmon fillets**, skinned
4 squares of **banana leaf**
    (about 30 cm/12 inches)
    square)
salt and **pepper**

Put the fresh coriander, mint, garlic, ginger, chillies,
cumin, ground coriander, sugar, lime juice and coconut
milk into a food processor or blender and blend until
fairly smooth. Season and set aside.

Place each salmon fillet on a square of banana leaf
and spoon some of the herb and spice mixture over it.
Carefully wrap the fish in the leaf to make a neat parcel
and secure with wooden skewers. If the banana leaves
are difficult to handle, dip them in boiling water for
15–20 seconds and they will become more supple.

Place the parcels on a large baking sheet and bake
in a preheated oven at 200°C (400°F), Gas Mark 6 for
15 minutes.

Remove the parcels from the oven, place on a serving
plate and open the packages at the table.

For swordfish parcels, make the parcels from baking
paper or foil instead of banana leaves. Use 4 × 175 g
(6 oz) portions swordfish instead of salmon. Prepare
as above and bake in a preheated oven at 180°C
(350°F), Gas Mark 4, for 20–25 minutes. **Calories
per serving 242**

spicy goan aubergine curry

Calories per serving **367**
Serves **4**
Preparation time **15 minutes**
Cooking time **about 25
minutes**

1 teaspoon **cumin seeds**
4 teaspoons **coriander seeds**
1 teaspoon **cayenne pepper**
2 **fresh green chillies,**
deseeded and sliced
½ teaspoon **ground turmeric**
4 **garlic cloves**, crushed
1 tablespoon peeled and
grated **fresh root ginger**
300 ml (½ pint) **warm water**
400 ml (14 fl oz) can **reduced-
fat coconut milk**
1 tablespoon **tamarind paste**
1 large **aubergine**, thinly sliced
lengthways
salt and **pepper**

Dry-roast the cumin and coriander seeds in a nonstick frying pan over a low heat for 2–3 minutes until fragrant. Remove from the heat and crush them lightly. Place them in a large saucepan with the cayenne, chillies, turmeric, garlic, ginger and the measured warm water.

Bring to the boil, reduce the heat and simmer for 10 minutes until thickened. Season to taste. Stir in the coconut milk and tamarind paste.

Arrange the aubergine slices in a foil-lined grill pan and brush the tops with some of the curry sauce. Cook under a preheated hot grill, turning once, until golden and tender. Serve the aubergine slices in the curry sauce with 1 chapati per person.

For cashew and courgette curry, add 200 g (7 oz) roasted cashew nuts to the finished curry sauce. To roast, soak in water for 20 minutes, chop, then heat in a dry frying pan, shaking regularly, until lightly browned. Replace the aubergine with 4 sliced courgettes and grill as above. Season to taste.
Calories per serving 438

bhoona chicken curry

Calories per serving **370**
Serves **4**
Preparation time **10 minutes,
    plus marinating**
Cooking time **8–10 minutes**

125 ml (4 fl oz) **fat-free
    natural yogurt**
juice of 2 **limes**
2 **garlic cloves**, finely chopped
1 teaspoon **ground turmeric**
1 tablespoon **mild chilli
    powder**
1 teaspoon **cardamom seeds**,
    crushed
large pinch of **sea salt**
1 tablespoon **ground
    coriander**
1 tablespoon **ground cumin**
4 skinless **chicken breast
    fillets**, cut into strips
1 tablespoon **groundnut oil**
1 teaspoon **garam masala**
    (see page 80)
handful of roughly chopped
    fresh coriander leaves
150 g (5 oz) steamed **rice**
    per person, to serve

Place the yogurt, lime juice, garlic, turmeric, chilli powder, cardamom, salt, ground coriander and cumin in a large non-metallic bowl. Mix well and add the chicken. Toss to coat evenly, cover and marinate in the refrigerator for 6–8 hours or overnight.

Heat the oil in a large nonstick frying pan over a medium-high heat, and stir-fry the chicken mixture for 8–10 minutes until tender and cooked through.

Sprinkle over the garam masala and chopped coriander, stir well and serve with the steamed rice.

For masala chicken kebabs, prepare the marinade as above and add 4 skinless chicken breast fillets, cut into cubes. Marinate in the refrigerator for 6–8 hours or overnight if time permits. When ready to cook, thread the chicken pieces on to 8 metal skewers and cook under a medium-hot grill for 5–6 minutes on each side or until cooked through. Serve with ½ a large, warmed naan bread per person. **Calories per serving 367**

bangkok sour pork curry

Calories per serving **374**
Serves **4**
Preparation time **20 minutes**
Cooking time **2¼ hours**

1 tablespoon **groundnut oil**
1 **onion**, finely chopped
1 teaspoon peeled and finely
  grated **galangal**
3 tablespoons **Thai red curry
  paste**
750 g (1 ½ lb) thick **pork
  steaks**, cubed
750 ml (1 ¼ pints) **chicken
  stock**
8 tablespoons finely chopped
  fresh coriander root and
  stem
2 **lemon grass stalks**, bruised
4 tablespoons **tamarind paste**
1 tablespoon **palm sugar** or
  brown sugar
6 **kaffir lime leaves**
small handful of **Thai basil
  leaves**, to garnish

Preheat the oven to 150°C (300°F), Gas Mark 2.
Heat the oil in a large casserole and fry the onion over
a medium heat for 3–4 minutes. Add the galangal,
curry paste and pork and stir-fry for 4–5 minutes.

Pour in the stock and add the chopped coriander,
lemon grass, tamarind, sugar and lime leaves. Bring
to the boil, cover and cook in the preheated oven for
2 hours or until the pork is tender.

Garnish with Thai basil and serve.

For Bangkok sour pork curry with noodles, cook
250 g (8 oz) thick egg noodles according to packet
instructions. Fresh noodles, available in the chilled
section of Oriental stores and large supermarkets,
have the best texture, but dried noodles are a good
substitute. Divide the noodles between 4 warmed
bowls and ladle the curry, cooked as above, over the
top. Sprinkle with chopped coriander leaves as well
as the Thai basil. **Calories per serving 487**

fragrant vietnamese beef curry

Calories per serving **384**
Serves **4**
Preparation time **15 minutes**
Cooking time **20–25 minutes**

2 tablespoons **groundnut oil**
750 g (1½ lb) **thin-cut fillet steak**, trimmed of fat and cut into strips
1 **onion**, finely sliced
4 **garlic cloves**, crushed
1 **fresh red chilli**, finely sliced
2 **star anise**
1 teaspoon **cardamom seeds**, crushed
1 **cinnamon stick**
300 g (10 oz) **French beans**, trimmed
1 **carrot**, cut into batons
2 tablespoons **Thai fish sauce**
2 tablespoons **ground bean sauce**

To garnish
small handful of finely chopped **fresh coriander leaves**
small handful of finely chopped **mint leaves**

Heat half the oil in a large nonstick frying pan and stir-fry the beef in batches for 1–2 minutes. Remove with a slotted spoon and keep warm.

Heat the remaining oil in the frying pan and stir-fry the onion for 4–5 minutes until softened, then add the garlic, chilli, star anise, cardamom, cinnamon, beans and carrot. Stir-fry for 6–8 minutes.

Return the beef to the pan with the fish sauce and ground bean sauce. Stir-fry for 3–4 minutes or until heated through. Remove from the heat and sprinkle over the chopped herbs just before serving.

For fresh beef spring rolls, soak 8 large rice paper wrappers in warm water for 3–4 minutes or until soft and pliable. Pat dry with kitchen paper and spread out on a clean work surface. Thinly shred 6 iceberg lettuce leaves and divide between the wrappers. Top each with 3 tablespoons of the beef curry, cooked as above, arranged in a neat pile along the middles of the wrappers. Turn up the bottom of the wrapper to cover the filling then carefully turn the two sides in and very gently roll up. Transfer to a serving plate and cover with a damp cloth while you make the remaining rolls. Serve immediately or the wrappers will dry out and become tough. **Calories per serving 335**

red fish, broccoli & bean curry

Calories per serving **385**
  (not including rice)
Serves **4**
Preparation time **15 minutes**
Cooking time **10 minutes**

1 tablespoon **groundnut oil**
1½–2 tablespoons **Thai red
  curry paste**
200 ml (7 fl oz) **coconut
  cream**
250 ml (8 fl oz) **vegetable
  stock**
1 tablespoon **tamarind paste**
1 tablespoon **Thai fish sauce**
1 tablespoon **palm sugar** or
  brown sugar
200 g (7 oz) **broccoli florets**
200 g (7 oz) **French beans**,
  cut into 2.5 cm (1 inch)
  lengths
450 g (14½ oz) **thick white
  fish fillet**, skinned and cubed
150 g (5 oz) can **bamboo
  shoots**, drained (optional)
small handful of **Thai basil
  leaves**, to garnish
lime wedges, to serve

Heat the oil in a large wok or frying pan over a medium
heat, add the curry paste and stir-fry for 1–2 minutes.
Stir in the coconut cream, stock, tamarind paste, fish
sauce and sugar and bring to the boil, then reduce the
heat and simmer gently for a further 2–3 minutes.

Add the broccoli and beans and simmer gently for
2 minutes. Stir in the fish and simmer gently for a
further 3–4 minutes or until just cooked through.
Stir in the bamboo shoots, if using.

Ladle into warmed bowls, sprinkle with Thai basil and
serve with lime wedges and boiled rice, if liked.

For Thai mixed seafood curry, replace the broccoli
and French beans with 1 large thinly sliced carrot and
1 thinly sliced red pepper. Follow the recipe above,
omitting the fish, but adding 12 raw king prawns, peeled
and deveined, 125 g (4 oz) prepared squid rings and
500 g (1 lb) scrubbed and debearded mussels. Simmer
gently until the mussels open, discarding any that do
not. Add 200 g (7 oz) fresh or canned pineapple chunks
instead of the bamboo shoots and serve as above.
Calories per serving 368 (not including rice)

thai jungle curry with duck

Calories per serving **389**
Serves **4**
Preparation time **20 minutes**
Cooking time **30 minutes**

2 tablespoons **Thai green
curry paste** (see page 208)
2 tablespoons finely chopped
lemon grass (tough outer
leaves removed)
3 **kaffir lime leaves**, finely
shredded
1 teaspoon **shrimp paste**
6 **garlic cloves**, crushed
5 **shallots**, finely chopped
3 tablespoons finely chopped
coriander root
2 tablespoons **groundnut oil**
cooking oil spray
625 g (1¼ lb) **skinless duck
breast fillets**, thinly sliced
400 ml (14 fl oz) **chicken
stock**
1 tablespoon **Thai fish sauce**
65 g (2½ oz) canned **bamboo
shoots**, rinsed and drained
4 **baby aubergines**, quartered
small handful of **Thai basil
leaves**

Place the green curry paste, lemon grass, lime leaves, shrimp paste, garlic, shallots, coriander root and groundnut oil in a mini blender and blend to a smooth paste, adding a little water if necessary.

Spray a large nonstick wok with cooking oil spray, place over a high heat and add the curry paste. Stir-fry for 1–2 minutes, then add the duck. Stir-fry for 4–5 minutes until sealed, then pour in the stock and fish sauce and bring to the boil. Remove the duck from the pan with a slotted spoon, set aside and keep warm.

Add the bamboo shoots and aubergines to the pan and cook for 12–15 minutes or until tender.

Return the meat to the pan and cook gently for 3–4 minutes. Stir in half the basil leaves and remove from the heat. Ladle into bowls, and garnish with the remaining basil.

For jungle curry with pigeon, replace the duck with 8 pigeon breasts, thinly sliced. Follow the recipe above, using light soy sauce instead of Thai fish sauce, and replacing the bamboo shoots with canned water chestnuts for a crunchy texture. Cook as above until the pigeon is tender. **Calories per serving 409**

curried tofu with vegetables

Calories per serving **393**
Serves **4**
Preparation time **20 minutes**
Cooking time **25 minutes**

2 tablespoons **sunflower oil**
2 teaspoons finely **grated fresh root ginger**
8 **garlic cloves**, chopped
8 **small shallots**, chopped
1 teaspoon **ground turmeric**
2 **fresh red chillies**, chopped
4 tablespoons very finely chopped **lemon grass**
400 ml (14 fl oz) can **coconut milk**
200 ml (7 fl oz) **vegetable stock**
4 **lime leaves**, finely shredded
12 **baby courgettes**, cut in half lengthways
12 **baby sweetcorn**, trimmed and cut in half lengthways
400 g (13 oz) **firm tofu**, cut into bite-sized cubes
1 tablespoon **dark soy sauce**
1 tablespoon **lime juice**
salt and **pepper**
small handful of roughly chopped **fresh coriander**

Place the oil, ginger, garlic, shallots, turmeric, chillies, lemon grass and half the coconut milk in a food processor and process until fairly smooth.

Heat a large nonstick wok and pour the coconut mixture into it. Stir-fry over a high heat for 3–4 minutes and then add the remaining coconut milk, the stock and lime leaves. Bring to the boil, reduce the heat and simmer gently, uncovered, for 10 minutes.

Add the courgettes and baby sweetcorn to the mixture and simmer for 6–7 minutes. Stir in the tofu, soy sauce and lime juice, season to taste and cook gently for 1–2 minutes.

Remove from the heat and stir in the fresh coriander. Serve in bowls garnished with basil leaves.

For pattypan curry with seafood, replace the baby courgettes and sweetcorn with pattypan squash, and use reduced-fat coconut milk. Cook as above. Replace the tofu with 16–20 raw tiger prawns and 500 g (1 lb) squid rings. Add the prawns and squid to the curry with the vegetables and finish as above. **Calories per serving 343**

cumin lentils with yogurt dressing

Calories per serving **398**
Serves **4**
Preparation time **10 minutes**
Cooking time **13 minutes**

4 tablespoons **olive oil**
2 **red onions**, thinly sliced
2 **garlic cloves**, chopped
2 teaspoons **cumin seeds**
500 g (1 lb) cooked **Puy lentils**
125 g (4 oz) **peppery leaves**, such as beetroot or rocket
1 large **raw beetroot**, peeled and coarsely grated
1 **Granny Smith apple**, peeled and coarsely grated (optional)
lemon juice, to serve
salt and **pepper**

Yogurt dressing
300 ml (½ pint) **Greek yogurt**
2 tablespoons **lemon juice**
½ teaspoon **ground cumin**
15 g (½ oz) **mint leaves**, chopped

Heat the oil in a frying pan and fry the red onions over a medium heat for about 8 minutes until soft and golden. Add the garlic and cumin seeds and cook for a further 5 minutes.

Mix the onion mixture into the lentils, season well and leave to cool.

Make the yogurt dressing by mixing together the ingredients in a small bowl.

Serve the cooled lentils on a bed of leaves, with the grated beetroot and apple (if used), a couple of spoonfuls of minty yogurt and a generous squeeze of lemon juice.

For cumin chickpeas with apricots, use 2 × 425 g (14 oz) cans chickpeas instead of the lentils. Chop and add 100 g (3½ oz) ready-to-eat dried apricots to replace the beetroot and apple. **Calories per serving 414**

monkfish & sweet potato curry

Calories per serving **399**
 (not including rice)
Serves **4**
Preparation time **15 minutes**
Cooking time **about**
 20 minutes

2 **lemon grass stalks**, roughly
 chopped
2 **shallots**, roughly chopped
1 **large red chilli**, deseeded
1 **garlic clove**
1.5 cm (¾ inch) piece of **fresh**
 root ginger, peeled and
 chopped
3 tablespoons **groundnut oil**
2 × 400 ml (14 fl oz) cans
 reduced-fat coconut milk
2 **sweet potatoes**, cut into
 1.5 cm (¾ inch) cubes
2 **large monkfish tails**, about
 250 g (8 oz) each, cut into
 large chunks
2 tablespoons **Thai fish sauce**
1 teaspoon **soft dark brown**
 sugar
1½ tablespoons **lime juice**
2 tablespoons roughly
 chopped **fresh coriander**,
 to garnish

Put the lemon grass, shallots, chilli, garlic, ginger and oil in a food processor or blender and blend to a smooth paste.

Heat a saucepan over a medium heat, add the paste and fry for 2 minutes until fragrant, then add the coconut milk. Bring to the boil and cook for 5 minutes until it reaches the consistency of cream. Add the sweet potatoes and cook until almost tender.

Add the monkfish and simmer for a further 5 minutes or until the fish is firm and cooked through. Add the fish sauce, sugar and lime juice, to taste. Sprinkle with the coriander. Serve with some Thai sticky rice, if liked.

For Thai-roasted monkfish with roasted chilli pumpkin, mix 2 tablespoons Thai red curry paste with 4 tablespoons fat-free natural yogurt in a non-metallic bowl. Add 2 monkfish tails, cut into large pieces, cover and leave to marinate in the refrigerator for at least 20 minutes or overnight if possible. Pan-fry the pieces of fish in a little vegetable oil until cooked through. Cut a 500 g (1 lb) pumpkin in half, scoop out the seeds, peel and cut into 2.5 cm (1 inch) cubes. Sprinkle with dried chilli flakes and roast in a preheated oven, 200°C (400°F), Gas Mark 6, for 15–20 minutes, or until tender, turning occasionally. Serve with extra natural yogurt mixed with chopped coriander. **Calories per serving 177**

thai red tofu & vegetable curry

Calories per serving **364**
(not including rice)
Serves **4**
Preparation time **15 minutes**
Cooking time **25–30 minutes**

450 g (14½ oz) **firm tofu**
1 tablespoon **rapeseed oil**
2 tablespoons ready-made
  Thai red curry paste
1–2 **fresh green chillies**,
  sliced
200 ml (7 fl oz) **reduced-fat**
  coconut milk
250 ml (8 fl oz) **vegetable**
  stock
1 large **aubergine**, diced
12 **baby sweetcorn**
100 g (3½ oz) **mangetout**
100 g (3½ oz) **carrots**, sliced
125 g (4 oz) **shiitake**
  mushrooms, halved
1 large **green pepper**, sliced
150 g (5 oz) canned **sliced**
  bamboo shoots, drained
1 tablespoon **Thai fish sauce**
1 tablespoon **clear honey**
2 **kaffir lime leaves**

To garnish
handful of **Thai basil leaves**
handful of **cashew nuts**,
  toasted

Drain the tofu and pat it dry with kitchen paper before cutting it into 5 cm (2 inch) cubes.

Heat the oil in a wok over a high heat until the oil starts to shimmer. Stir-fry the red curry paste and chillies for 1 minute, then stir in 2 tablespoons of the coconut milk (from the thicker part at the top of the can) and cook, stirring constantly, for 2 minutes.

Add the stock and bring to the boil. Add the aubergine, then bring the mixture back to the boil and simmer for about 5 minutes. Add the remaining vegetables and cook for another 5–10 minutes. Stir in the fish sauce, honey, lime leaves and the remaining coconut milk and simmer for another 5 minutes, stirring occasionally. Add the tofu cubes and mix well.

Garnish with torn Thai basil leaves and toasted cashew nuts. Serve with jasmine or sticky (glutinous) rice, if liked, which will absorb the wonderful aromatic sauce.

For one-pot tofu & vegetable noodles, use 400 ml (14 fl oz) reduced-fat coconut milk and increase the quantity of stock to 350 ml (12 fl oz). Add 150 g (5 oz) cooked thick rice noodles along with the tofu and simmer for 1 minute before serving with the garnish above. **Calories per serving 499**

curried cauliflower with chickpeas

Calories per serving **310**
(**not including chapatis**)
Serves **4**
Preparation time **10 minutes**
Cooking time **20 minutes**

2 tablespoons **olive oil**
1 **onion**, chopped
2 **garlic cloves**, crushed
4 tablespoons **medium curry paste**
1 small **cauliflower**, divided into florets
375 ml (13 fl oz) **vegetable stock**
4 **tomatoes**, roughly chopped
400 g (13 oz) can **chickpeas**, rinsed and drained
2 tablespoons **mango chutney** (see right)
salt and **pepper**
4 tablespoons chopped **fresh coriander**, to garnish

Heat the oil in a saucepan, add the onion and garlic and cook until the onion is soft and starting to brown. Stir in the curry paste, add the cauliflower and stock and bring to the boil. Reduce the heat, cover tightly and simmer for 10 minutes.

Add the tomatoes, chickpeas and chutney and continue to cook, uncovered, for 10 minutes. Season to taste with salt and pepper. Garnish with coriander and serve with rolled chapatis, if liked.

For homemade mango chutney, put the peeled, stoned and sliced flesh of 6 ripe mangoes in a large saucepan with 300 ml (½ pint) white wine vinegar and cook over a low heat for 10 minutes. Add 250 g (8 oz) soft dark brown sugar, 50 g (2 oz) fresh root ginger, peeled and finely chopped, 2 crushed garlic cloves, 2 teaspoons chilli powder and 1 teaspoon salt and bring to the boil, stirring constantly. Reduce the heat and simmer for 30 minutes, stirring occasionally. Ladle into a sterilized screw-top jar and replace the lid. Store in the refrigerator and use within 1 month.
Calories per jar 449

spiced beef & vegetable stew

Calories per serving **325**
Serves **4**
Preparation time **15 minutes**
Cooking time **2½ hours**

500 g (1 lb) **lean braising** or
  stewing steak
2 tablespoons **rapeseed** or
  olive oil
1 large **onion**, chopped
2.5 cm (1 inch) piece of **fresh
  root ginger**, peeled and
  finely grated
2 **chillies**, sliced
2 **garlic cloves**, crushed
600 ml (1 pint) **beef stock**
5 **star anise**
1 teaspoon **Chinese five-
  spice powder**
1 **cinnamon stick**
1 teaspoon **fennel seeds**
2 **dried kaffir lime leaves**
1 **lemon grass stalk**, chopped
1 teaspoon **black peppercorns**
2 tablespoons **shoyu** or
  tamari sauce
400 g (13 oz) **carrots**, cut into
  1 cm (½ inch) slices
500 g (1 lb) **mooli** or **turnips**,
  cut into 1 cm (½ inch) slices
Chinese chives or **regular
  chives**, to garnish

Cut the steak into 2.5 cm (1 inch) cubes.

Heat the oil in a wok over a medium heat. Add the onion, ginger and chillies and stir-fry for 5–7 minutes.

Turn the heat up to high, add the beef and stir-fry for 5–10 minutes until lightly browned, stirring occasionally.

Add the garlic, stock, star anise, Chinese five-spice powder, cinnamon, fennel seeds, lime leaves, lemon grass, peppercorns and shoyu sauce and stir well. Bring the mixture back to the boil, then turn the heat down, cover the pan and simmer gently for 1½ hours, stirring occasionally. Add the carrots and mooli and continue cooking, covered, for another 45 minutes or until the vegetables have softened.

Skim any fat off the surface and garnish with the chives before serving.

For sesame broccoli, to accompany the stew, blanch 500 g (1 lb) broccoli florets in a saucepan of boiling water for 2 minutes, then drain and place on a serving dish. Make a dressing by combining 1 teaspoon sesame oil, 1 tablespoon shoyu sauce and 1 crushed garlic clove, and pour it over the broccoli. Just before serving, sprinkle the dish with 1 tablespoon toasted sesame seeds. **Calories per serving 69**

strawberry lassi

Approximate calories per
serving **375**
Makes **1.5 litres (2½ pints)**

400 g (13 oz) **strawberries**
750 ml (1 ¼ pints) **ice-cold water**
300 ml (½ pint) **low-fat live natural yogurt**
25 g (1 oz) **golden caster sugar**
few drops of **rosewater**
coarsely ground **black pepper**, to serve

Hull and roughly chop the strawberries. Put the strawberries in a food processor or blender with half the water and process until smooth.

Add the yogurt, sugar, rosewater and the remaining water and process again until smooth and frothy.

Pour the smoothie into chilled glasses, sprinkle with black pepper and serve immediately.

For banana lassi, process 2 small ripe bananas with 300 ml (½ pint) live natural yogurt, 125 ml (4 fl oz) ice-cold water and a pinch of ground cardamom in a food processor or blender. **Calories per 6 servings 382**

recipes
under 500
calories

spiced halibut curry

Calories per serving **404**
  (not including yogurt)
Serves **4**
Preparation time **15 minutes,
  plus chilling**
Cooking time **40–50 minutes**

60 ml (2½ fl oz) **lemon juice**
60 ml (2½ fl oz) **rice wine
  vinegar**
2 tablespoons **cumin seeds**
1 teaspoon **chilli powder**
1 teaspoon **ground turmeric**
1 teaspoon **salt**
750 g (1½ lb) thick **halibut
  fillets**, skinned and cut
  into cubes
4 tablespoons **sunflower oil**
1 **onion**, finely chopped
3 **garlic cloves**, crushed
2 tablespoons finely grated
  fresh root ginger
2 teaspoons **black mustard
  seeds**
2 × 400 g (13 oz) cans
  chopped tomatoes
1 teaspoon **sugar**

To garnish
chopped **fresh coriander**
sliced **fresh green chillies**
natural yogurt (optional)

Mix together the lemon juice, rice wine vinegar, cumin, chilli powder, turmeric and salt in a non-metallic bowl. Add the fish and turn to coat evenly. Cover and chill for 25–30 minutes.

Meanwhile, heat a wok over a high heat and add the oil. When hot, add the onion, garlic, ginger and mustard seeds. Reduce the heat and cook gently for 10 minutes, stirring occasionally.

Add the tomatoes and sugar, bring to the boil, reduce the heat, cover and cook gently for 15–20 minutes, stirring occasionally.

Add the fish and its marinade, stir gently to mix and then cover and simmer gently for 15–20 minutes or until the fish is cooked through and flakes easily.

Garnish with chopped fresh coriander and green chillies and drizzle over some natural yogurt, if desired.

For dry-spiced haddock, use 750 g (1½ lb) haddock fillets instead of halibut, cutting the fillets into large chunks. Heat a wok over a high heat and pour in the sunflower oil. When hot, add the onion, garlic, fresh root ginger and black mustard seeds. Add the fish and cook for 5 minutes until just firm, turning occasionally. Add 2–3 tablespoons water and cook for 3–5 minutes. Serve drizzled with yogurt, if desired, and sprinkled with coriander. **Calories per serving 307 (not including yogurt)**

monkfish korma

Calories per serving **405**
Serves **4**
Preparation time **10 minutes**
Cooking time **20 minutes**

1 tablespoon **groundnut oil**
2 tablespoons **korma curry powder**
750 g (1½ lb) **monkfish fillet**, cubed
large bunch of **fresh coriander leaves**, finely chopped
1 **red onion**, finely chopped
finely grated rind and juice of 2 **limes**
400 ml (14 fl oz) can **reduced-fat coconut milk**
salt and **pepper**
150 g (5 oz) steamed **rice** per person, to serve

Heat the oil in a wide saucepan over a medium heat. Add the curry powder and stir-fry for 20–30 seconds or until fragrant. Add the monkfish, coriander and red onion and cook, stirring, for a further 20–30 seconds.

Add the lime rind and juice and the coconut milk. Bring to the boil, reduce the heat and simmer for 15 minutes or until the fish is cooked through. Season to taste and serve immediately with the steamed rice.

For monkfish Madras, replace the korma curry powder with Madras curry powder, and the coconut milk with 200 ml (7 fl oz) tomato passata and 200 ml (7 fl oz) fish stock. Cook as above until the fish is cooked through. Serve with 1 chapati per person. **Calories per serving 451**

sri lankan-style lamb curry

Calories per serving **409**
Serves **4**
Preparation time **10 minutes**
Cooking time **35 minutes**

500 g (1 lb) **boneless shoulder** or **leg of lamb**, diced
2 **potatoes**, cut into large chunks
4 tablespoons **olive oil**
400 g (13 oz) can **chopped tomatoes**
150 ml (¼ pint) **water**
salt and **pepper**

Curry paste
1 **onion**, grated
1 tablespoon peeled and finely chopped **fresh root ginger**
1 teaspoon finely chopped **garlic**
½ teaspoon **ground turmeric**
1 teaspoon **ground coriander**
½ teaspoon **ground cumin**
½ teaspoon **fennel seeds**
½ teaspoon **cumin seeds**
3 **cardamom pods**, crushed
2 **fresh green chillies**, finely diced
5 cm (2 inch) **cinnamon stick**
2 **lemon grass stalks**, thinly sliced

Make the curry paste. Mix together all the ingredients in a large bowl. (For a milder curry, remove the seeds from the chillies before dicing.) Add the lamb and potatoes and mix well.

Heat the oil in a heavy-based saucepan or flameproof casserole, tip in the lamb and potato mixture and cook, stirring, for 6–8 minutes.

Stir in the tomatoes and measurement water and bring to the boil. Season well with salt and pepper, then reduce the heat and simmer for 20–25 minutes until the potatoes are cooked and the lamb is tender.

For beef & potato curry, use 500 g (1 lb) rump steak, cut into chunks, instead of the lamb. Cook the recipe as above and then serve with a generous sprinkling of chopped fresh coriander. **Calories per serving 435**

swahili chicken

Calories per serving **412 (not including rice or flat bread)**

Serves **4**

Preparation time **20 minutes, plus marinating**

Cooking time **1½ hours**

1 **chicken**, cut into 8 pieces

4 teaspoons finely **grated fresh root ginger**

6 **garlic cloves**, crushed

2 teaspoons **ground turmeric**

1 tablespoon **paprika**

1 teaspoon **ground cinnamon**

8 tablespoons **lemon juice**

4 tablespoons **sunflower oil**

2 teaspoons **ground cumin**

1 tablespoon **ground coriander**

2 teaspoons **dried chilli flakes**

100 g (3½ oz) **natural yogurt**, whisked

1 tablespoon **runny honey**

salt and **pepper**

Place the chicken pieces in a large mixing bowl. Mix together the remaining ingredients, season well and pour over the chicken. Mix well to combine, cover and marinate in the refrigerator for 6–8 hours or overnight if time permits.

Place the chicken mixture in a shallow, lightly oiled, ovenproof baking dish and cook in a preheated oven at 150°C (300°F), Gas Mark 2 for 1½ hours, covering the dish with foil for the last 30–40 minutes of cooking. Serve accompanied by plain boiled rice or flat bread, if liked.

For Swahili chicken drumsticks with cumin dip,

use 12 small chicken drumsticks instead of the whole chicken and proceed as above. To make it easier to eat the drumsticks with your fingers, only cover the chicken with foil when the dish is quite dry. Serve at room temperature with minted yogurt for dipping. To make this, whisk 250 g (8 oz) natural yogurt with ¼ teaspoon ground cumin and 4 tablespoons finely chopped fresh mint. Season well then chill until ready to serve.
Calories per serving 405

fast chicken curry

Calories per serving **413**
Serves **4**
Preparation time **5 minutes**
Cooking time **20–25 minutes**

3 tablespoons **olive oil**
1 **onion**, finely chopped
4 tablespoons **medium curry paste**
8 boneless, skinless **chicken thighs**, cut into thin strips
400 g (13 oz) can **chopped tomatoes**
250 g (8 oz) **broccoli**, broken into small florets, stalks peeled and sliced
100 ml (3½ fl oz) **reduced-fat coconut milk**
salt and **pepper**

Heat the oil in a deep nonstick saucepan over a medium heat. Add the onion and cook for 3 minutes until soft and translucent. Add the curry paste and cook, stirring, for 1 minute until fragrant.

Add the chicken, tomatoes, broccoli and coconut milk to the pan. Bring to the boil, then reduce the heat, cover and simmer gently over a low heat for 15–20 minutes until the chicken is cooked through.

Remove from the heat, season well with salt and pepper and serve immediately.

For chicken patties with curry sauce, follow the first stage of the recipe above, then add the tomatoes, 200 g (7 oz) young spinach leaves and the reduced-fat coconut milk (omitting the chicken and broccoli), and cook as directed. Meanwhile, finely chop 450 g (1 lb) cooked chicken breasts. Transfer to a bowl and add 4 finely chopped spring onions, 2 tablespoons chopped fresh coriander, 50 g (2 oz) fresh white breadcrumbs, a squeeze of lemon juice and 1 beaten egg. Season with salt and pepper. Mix well, then form into 16 patties. Roll in 25 g (1 oz) fresh white breadcrumbs to coat. Brush vegetable oil around a large frying pan over a medium heat. Add the patties, cooking in batches, and pan-fry on each side until golden brown and cooked through. Serve hot with the curry sauce. **Calories per serving 490**

chicken & baby spinach curry

Calories per serving **420**
Serves **4**
Preparation time **10 minutes**
Cooking time **25 minutes**

1 tablespoon **sunflower oil**
4 **boneless, skinless chicken breasts**, halved lengthways
1 **onion**, sliced
2 **garlic cloves**, chopped
1 **green chilli**, chopped
4 **cardamom pods**, lightly crushed
1 teaspoon **cumin seeds**
1 teaspoon **dried chilli flakes**
1 teaspoon **ground ginger**
1 teaspoon **ground turmeric**
250 g (8 oz) **baby leaf spinach**
300 g (10 oz) **tomatoes**, chopped
150 g (5 oz) **natural yogurt**
2 tablespoons chopped **fresh coriander**
150 g (5 oz) steamed **rice** per person, to serve

Heat the oil in a large nonstick saucepan or frying pan. Add the chicken, onion, garlic and chilli and fry for 4–5 minutes until the chicken begins to brown and the onion to soften.

Add the cardamom pods, cumin seeds, chilli flakes, ginger and turmeric and continue to fry for 1 minute.

Add the spinach to the pan, cover and cook gently until the spinach wilts, then stir in the tomatoes and simmer for 15 minutes, removing the lid for the last 5 minutes.

Stir in the yogurt and chopped coriander and serve with the steamed rice.

For chicken & pea curry, use 200 g (7 oz) fresh or frozen peas, adding them to the curry with the tomatoes. Sprinkle with 1 tablespoon chopped fresh mint as well as the coriander before serving. **Calories per serving 458**

curry leaf & tomato prawns

Calories per serving **427**
Serves **4**
Preparation time **15 minutes**
Cooking time **15–20 minutes**

1 tablespoon **groundnut oil**
10–12 **curry leaves**
2 **large shallots**, halved and
  finely sliced
2 teaspoons finely grated
  garlic
1 teaspoon peeled and finely
  grated **fresh root ginger**
1 tablespoon **fennel seeds**
1 tablespoon **medium curry
  powder**
6 **large ripe tomatoes**,
  peeled, deseeded and
  chopped
750 g (1½ lb) **raw tiger prawns**,
  peeled and deveined
salt
150 g (5 oz) steamed **rice** per
  person, to serve

Heat the oil in a large wok or frying pan over a medium heat. Add the curry leaves and stir-fry for 30 seconds. Add the shallots and stir-fry for a further 4–5 minutes.

Add the garlic, ginger and fennel seeds, reduce the heat and cook gently for 2–3 minutes. Sprinkle over the curry powder and add the tomatoes, including any juices. Increase the heat and stir-fry for 3–4 minutes.

Add the prawns and continue cooking over a high heat for 6–7 minutes until the prawns turn pink and are just cooked through. Remove from the heat, season to taste and serve immediately with the rice or crushed sesame spiced potatoes.

For crushed sesame spiced potatoes, to serve as an accompaniment, peel 4 medium potatoes and cut into 1 cm (½ inch) dice. Boil for 12 minutes or until just tender, then drain thoroughly. Heat 1 tablespoon groundnut oil in a large frying pan over a high heat. Add 1 tablespoon sesame seeds, 2 teaspoons cumin seeds, 2 teaspoons red chilli powder, ¼ teaspoon ground turmeric and the potatoes and stir-fry for 6–8 minutes, crushing them lightly with the back of a spoon. Season and serve. **Calories per serving 366**

burmese chicken noodle curry

Calories per serving **403**
Serves **6**
Preparation time **20 minutes**
Cooking time **about 1 hour**

1 kg (2 lb) boneless, skinless
  chicken thighs, cut into
  bite-sized pieces
2 **onions**, chopped
5 **garlic cloves**, chopped
1 teaspoon finely grated **fresh
  root ginger**
2 tablespoons **sunflower oil**
½ teaspoon **Burmese shrimp
  paste** (belacan)
400 ml (14 fl oz) can **coconut
  milk**
1 tablespoon **medium curry
  powder**
300 g (10½ oz) **dried rice
  vermicelli**
salt and **pepper**

To garnish
chopped **fresh coriander**
finely chopped **red onion**
fried **garlic slivers**
sliced **fresh red chillies**
lime wedges

Season the chicken pieces and set aside. Process the onion, garlic and ginger in a food processor until smooth. If necessary, add a little water to assist in blending the mixture. Heat the oil in a large pan. Add the onion mixture and shrimp paste and cook, stirring, over a high heat for about 5 minutes.

Add the chicken and cook over a medium heat, turning it until it browns.

Pour in the coconut milk and add the curry powder. Bring to the boil, reduce the heat and simmer, covered, for about 30 minutes, stirring from time to time. Uncover the pan and cook for a further 15 minutes or until the chicken is tender and cooked through.

Place the noodles in a bowl, cover with boiling water and set aside for 10 minutes. Drain the noodles and divide them between 4 large warmed serving bowls. Ladle over the curry, and garnish with chopped coriander, chopped red onion, fried garlic slivers, sliced red chillies and lime wedges.

For tofu noodle curry, replace the chicken with 450 g (14½ oz) cubed tofu, then add 50 g (1¾ oz) each of baby sweetcorn and mangetout to the curry 5 minutes before the end of cooking. Finish as above.
Calories per serving 313

malay beef with peanut sauce

Calories per serving **435**
Serves **6**
Preparation time **10 minutes**
Cooking time **15 minutes**

500 g (1 lb) **sirloin** or **rump
  steak**, thinly sliced
1 tablespoon **vegetable oil**

Marinade
½ teaspoon **turmeric**
1 teaspoon **ground cumin**
½ teaspoon **fennel seeds**
1 **bay leaf**, finely shredded
½ teaspoon **ground cinnamon**
75 ml (3 fl oz) **coconut cream**

Rice
250 g (8 oz) **Thai jasmine rice**
200 ml (7 fl oz) **reduced-fat
  coconut milk**
½ teaspoon **salt**

Peanut sauce
2 tablespoons **crunchy
  peanut butter**
¼ teaspoon **cayenne pepper**
1 tablespoon **light soy sauce**
125 ml (4 fl oz) **coconut cream**
½ teaspoon **caster sugar**

Make the marinade by mixing together all the ingredients in a non-metallic bowl. Add the beef, mix thoroughly, then thread the beef on to skewers and set aside to marinate.

Put the rice, coconut milk, salt and 250 ml (8 fl oz) water in a rice cooker or a covered saucepan over a low heat. Cook for about 15 minutes until the rice is cooked and the liquid has been absorbed.

Meanwhile, add the ingredients for the peanut sauce to a small saucepan with 3 tablespoons water and heat gently, stirring.

Heat the oil in a large frying pan and cook the beef skewers for about 5 minutes, turning so that each side is browned evenly. Serve immediately with the rice and peanut sauce.

For bean sprout & carrot salad to serve as an accompaniment, coarsely grate 4 carrots, roughly chop 4 spring onions and combine with 200 g (7 oz) bean sprouts. **Calories per serving 58**

spicy cod & tomato curry

Calories per serving **435**
Serves **4**
Preparation time **15 minutes**
Cooking time **40–50 minutes**

60 ml (2½ fl oz) **lemon juice**
60 ml (2½ fl oz) **rice wine vinegar**
2 tablespoons **cumin seeds**
2 tablespoons **hot curry powder**
large pinch of **salt**
750 g (1½ lb) thick **cod fillet**, skinned and cubed
1 tablespoon **groundnut oil**
1 **onion**, finely chopped
3 **garlic cloves**, finely chopped
2 teaspoons peeled and finely grated **fresh root ginger**
2 × 400 g (13 oz) cans **chopped tomatoes**
1 teaspoon **agave syrup**
150 g (5 oz) boiled **rice** per person, to serve

Mix the lemon juice with the rice wine vinegar, cumin seeds, curry powder and salt in a shallow non-metallic bowl. Add the fish and turn to coat evenly. Cover and marinate in the refrigerator for 25–30 minutes.

Meanwhile, heat a wok or large frying pan with a lid over a high heat and add the oil. When the oil is hot, add the onion, garlic and ginger. Reduce the heat and cook gently for 10 minutes, stirring occasionally.

Add the tomatoes and agave syrup, stir well and bring to the boil. Reduce the heat, cover and cook gently for 15–20 minutes, stirring occasionally.

Add the fish and its marinade, and stir gently to mix. Cover and simmer gently for 15–20 minutes until the fish is cooked through. Ladle into shallow bowls and serve with the boiled rice.

For cod & tomato biryani, place 1 tablespoon medium curry powder in a medium saucepan with 1 bay leaf, 1 cinnamon stick, a large pinch of saffron, 4 crushed cardamom pods, 3 cloves, 6 tablespoons tomato purée and 300 g (10 oz) basmati rice. Pour in 650 ml (1 pint 2 fl oz) hot fish stock, season and stir to mix well. Bring back to the boil and gently stir in 400 g (13 oz) skinless cod fillet chunks. Reduce the heat to low, cover the pan and cook gently for 10–12 minutes or until all the liquid has been absorbed. Remove from the heat and allow to stand, covered and undisturbed, for 10–15 minutes. Fluff up the grains with a fork and serve. **Calories per serving 413**

thai monkfish & prawn curry

Calories per serving **446**
Serves **4**
Preparation time **10 minutes**
Cooking time **8 minutes**

3 tablespoons **Thai green
curry paste** (see page 208)
400 ml (14 fl oz) can **reduced-
fat coconut milk**
1 **lemon grass stalk**
(optional), halved lengthwise
2 **kaffir lime leaves** (fresh or
dried, optional)
1 tablespoon **soft brown
sugar**
300 g (10 oz) **monkfish or
cod loins,** cubed
50 g (2 oz) **green beans**,
trimmed
12 raw peeled **tiger prawns**
2–3 tablespoons **Thai fish
sauce**
2 tablespoons fresh **lime juice**
150 g (5 oz) boiled **rice** per
person, to serve

To garnish
fresh coriander sprigs
sliced **fresh green chillies**

Put the curry paste and coconut milk in a saucepan.
Bruise the lemon grass stalk, by bashing with a rolling
pin, and add it to the pan with lime leaves, if using, and
sugar. Bring to the boil, then add the monkfish. Simmer
gently for 2 minutes, then add the beans and cook for
a further 2 minutes or until the fish is cooked through.

Stir in the prawns, fish sauce and lime juice and cook
for 2–5 minutes until the prawns turn pink and are
cooked through.

Transfer the curry to a warm serving dish and top
with coriander sprigs and chilli slices. Serve with plain
boiled rice.

For Malaysian monkfish & prawn curry, heat
2 tablespoons sunflower oil in a saucepan, add 2 thinly
sliced onions and fry gently until softened. Replace
the curry paste with 2 tablespoons lemon grass paste,
1 tablespoon garlic paste, 1 deseeded and diced red
chilli, 4 cm (1¾ inch) piece of fresh root ginger, peeled
and grated, 1 teaspoon turmeric, 1 cinnamon stick and
2 star anise and add to the onions with the reduced-
fat coconut milk, lemon grass and lime leaves, if using,
sugar and salt. Continue as above. **Calories per
serving 461**

mango & prawn curry

Calories per serving **447**
Serves **4**
Preparation time **10 minutes**
Cooking time **20–25 minutes**

3 **garlic cloves**, crushed
2 teaspoons peeled and finely
   grated **fresh root ginger**
2 tablespoons **ground**
   coriander
2 teaspoons **ground cumin**
1 teaspoon **chilli powder**
1 teaspoon **paprika**
½ teaspoon **ground turmeric**
1 tablespoon **palm sugar** or
   brown sugar
400 ml (14 fl oz) **water**
1 **green mango**, peeled,
   stoned and thinly sliced
400 ml (14 fl oz) can **reduced-**
   fat coconut milk
1 tablespoon **tamarind paste**
625 g (1 ¼ lb) raw **tiger**
   prawns, peeled and
   deveined
small bunch of **fresh coriander**
salt
150g (5 oz) boiled **rice** per
   person, to serve

Place the garlic, ginger, ground coriander, cumin, chilli powder, paprika, turmeric and sugar in a large wok or frying pan. Pour in the measured water and stir to mix well. Bring to the boil, reduce the heat and cook, covered, for 8–10 minutes.

Add the mango, coconut milk and tamarind paste and stir to combine. Bring the mixture back to the boil, then add the prawns. Reduce the heat and simmer gently for 6–8 minutes.

Tear half of the coriander leaves into the curry and cook for another 2 minutes until the prawns have turned pink and are just cooked through. Season to taste and serve immediately with the boiled rice, garnished with the remaining coriander.

For chicken & sweet potato curry, simmer the spices in the measured water as above. Omit the mango and prawns and add 1 small peeled and diced sweet potato and 500 g (1 lb) diced skinless chicken breast fillets with the coconut milk and tamarind paste. Bring to the boil, reduce the heat and simmer gently for 20 minutes until the chicken is cooked through. Add the coriander and serve as above. **Calories per serving 454**

scallops with spiced lentils

Calories per serving **451**
Serves **4**
Preparation time **10 minutes**
Cooking time **20–25 minutes**

250 g (8 oz) **red lentils**, rinsed
5 tablespoons **olive oil**
25 g (1 oz) **butter**
1 **onion**, finely chopped
1 **aubergine**, cut into 1 cm
   (½ inch) cubes
1 **garlic clove**, finely chopped
1 tablespoon **curry powder**
1 tablespoon chopped
   parsley, plus extra to garnish
12 cleaned **king scallops**,
   corals removed (optional)
salt and **pepper**

Cook the lentils in a saucepan of boiling water according to the packet instructions. Drain well.

Meanwhile, heat 1 tablespoon of the oil and the butter in a frying pan over a medium heat, add the onion and cook slowly for 10 minutes or until golden brown. Remove with a slotted spoon to a plate and turn the heat up to high. Add another 2 tablespoons of the oil to the pan and fry the aubergine in batches until coloured and softened.

Return the onion to the pan with the garlic, curry powder and cooked lentils and fry for a further minute to warm through. Season with salt and pepper and stir in the parsley.

Heat another frying pan over a high heat, then add the remaining oil. Season the scallops with salt and pepper, place them in the pan and cook for 1 minute on each side or until just cooked through. Serve immediately with the spiced lentils and garnish with parsley leaves.

For scallops with dhal & spinach, cook 250 g (8 oz) yellow split pea lentils according to the packet instructions and drain well. Heat a little vegetable oil in a frying pan, add the onion and garlic, omitting the aubergine, and fry until softened. Add 1 teaspoon curry powder, 1 teaspoon garam masala and a pinch of turmeric and fry for 1 minute. Add the cooked lentils with a little water or chicken stock to moisten the mixture. Add 500 g (1 lb) baby leaf spinach and stir until wilted. Cook the scallops as above with a light sprinkle of curry powder on each. Serve with the dhal.
Calories per serving 439

malaysian rendang lamb

Calories per serving **455**
Serves **6**
Preparation time **15 minutes**
Cooking time **2¾ hours**

2 tablespoons **sunflower oil**
800 g (1 lb 10 oz) **leg of
lamb**, butterflied
2 **onions**, finely chopped
1 tablespoon **ground
coriander**
1 teaspoon **ground turmeric**
6 **garlic cloves**, crushed
6 tablespoons very finely
chopped **lemon grass**
4–6 **bird's eye chillies**,
chopped
4 tablespoons finely chopped
fresh coriander root and
stem
400 ml (14 fl oz) can **reduced-
fat coconut milk**
salt and **pepper**

Heat the oil in a deep, heavy-based casserole dish and brown the lamb on both sides for about 5–6 minutes.

Place the remaining ingredients in a food processor and blend until smooth. Season well.

Pour this mixture over the lamb and bring to the boil. Cover tightly and cook in a preheated oven at 150°C (300°F), Gas Mark 2, turning the lamb occasionally, for 2½ hours or until the lamb is meltingly tender and most of the liquid has evaporated.

Remove from the oven and allow to stand for about 10–12 minutes before serving, cut into thick slices.

For winter salad, to serve as an accompaniment to this dish, mix together 300 g (10 oz) green cabbage, finely shredded, 1 carrot, coarsely grated and 1 red onion, finely sliced. In a separate dish mix together 3 tablespoons light olive oil and the juice of 1 lemon. Season the dressing well and pour over the salad mixture. Toss until the salad is thoroughly coated in the dressing and serve. **Calories per serving 131**

malaysian scallop & prawn curry

Calories per serving **456**
Serves **4**
Preparation time **20 minutes**
Cooking time **20–25 minutes**

1 tablespoon **chilli powder**
1 teaspoon **ground coriander**
2 teaspoons **ground cumin**
2 **garlic cloves**, crushed
1 **onion**, finely chopped
6 tablespoons finely chopped
  lemon grass
1 teaspoon **grated galangal**
  or **fresh root ginger**
1 tablespoon **grated palm**
  sugar
½ teaspoon **shrimp paste**
2 tablespoons finely chopped
  unroasted peanuts
600 ml (1 pint) **coconut milk**
200 g (7 oz) **green beans**,
  trimmed and halved
500 g (1 lb) **raw tiger prawns**
500 g (1 lb) **raw scallops**

To garnish
Thai basil leaves
4 teaspoons chopped
  unroasted peanuts
finely chopped **fresh red**
  chillies

Place the chilli powder, ground coriander, cumin, garlic, onion, lemon grass, galangal or ginger, palm sugar, shrimp paste, peanuts and coconut milk in a food processor and process until fairly smooth.

Place a large wok over a high heat and add the spice mixture. Bring to the boil, reduce the heat and simmer gently, uncovered, for 12–15 minutes, stirring occasionally.

Add the green beans, prawns and scallops and bring back to the boil. Reduce the heat and simmer gently for 6–8 minutes or until the prawns and scallops are cooked through.

Remove from the heat and scatter over some Thai basil leaves, chopped peanuts and chopped red chillies before serving.

For spicy squid & prawns, add 350 g (11½ oz) squid rings instead of the scallops and proceed as above. Serve with rice sticks or cellophane noodles instead of rice. **Calories per serving 392**

tindori & lentil curry

Calories per serving **463**
Serves **4**
Preparation time **15 minutes**
Cooking time **35 minutes**

125 g (4 oz) **green lentils**,
  rinsed
1 tablespoon **groundnut oil**
1 teaspoon **ground turmeric**
2 teaspoons **garam masala**
  (see page 80)
1 teaspoon **cumin seeds**
1 teaspoon **nigella seeds**
1 **fresh red chilli**, finely
  chopped
1 **fresh green chilli**, finely
  chopped
3 large **tomatoes**, chopped
250 g (8 oz) **tindori**, rinsed
  and trimmed
2 tablespoons **palm sugar** or
  brown sugar
1 tablespoon **tamarind paste**
150 ml (¼ pint) **boiling water**
4 warm **chapatis**
salt and **pepper**

Cook the lentils in a saucepan of boiling water for 20 minutes until soft. Drain well.

Meanwhile, heat the oil in a large saucepan and fry the turmeric, garam masala, cumin seeds and nigella seeds for 1–2 minutes or until the spices are sizzling. Add the chopped chillies, tomatoes, lentils and tindori and bring to the boil. Cover the pan, reduce the heat and simmer gently for 10 minutes, stirring occasionally.

Mix the sugar and tamarind paste with the boiling water and add to the pan. Stir well and simmer for a further 5 minutes. Season to taste and serve with 1 chapati per person and a green mango and red onion salad.

For green mango & red onion salad, to serve as an accompaniment, peel and stone 1 small green mango and finely shred the flesh. Mix with 1 small finely chopped red onion and a handful of coriander leaves. Cover and chill until required. **Calories per serving 36**

yellow salmon curry

Calories per serving **466**
Serves **4**
Preparation time **15 minutes**
Cooking time **25–30 minutes**

3 **garlic cloves**, finely grated
2 **fresh green chillies**,
   deseeded and finely
   chopped
2 teaspoons peeled and finely
   grated **fresh root ginger**
1 tablespoon **groundnut oil**
1 **onion**, finely chopped
1 tablespoon **ground turmeric**
200 ml (7 fl oz) **reduced-fat
   coconut milk**
200 ml (7 fl oz) **water**
2 **potatoes**, peeled and diced
4 thick **salmon steaks**, about
   175 g (6 oz) each
2 **tomatoes**, roughly chopped
salt
chopped **fresh coriander
   leaves**, to garnish

Pound the garlic, chillies and ginger with a pestle and mortar until you have a smooth paste.

Heat the oil in a large nonstick wok or saucepan over a medium heat. Add the paste and stir-fry for 2–3 minutes, then add the onion and turmeric. Stir-fry for a further 2–3 minutes until fragrant.

Stir in the coconut milk, measured water and the potatoes. Bring to the boil, reduce the heat to low and simmer gently for 10–12 minutes, stirring occasionally.

Season the fish with salt and add to the pan with the tomatoes. Bring the mixture back to the boil and simmer gently for 6–8 minutes until the fish is cooked through. Remove from the heat and garnish with chopped coriander.

For yellow mussel curry, replace the salmon with 1 kg (2 lb) mussels, which have been scrubbed and debearded. Cover the pan and cook over a high heat for 6–8 minutes or until the mussels have opened, discarding any that do not. Remove from the heat and garnish with chopped coriander. **Calories per serving 212**

chicken, okra & red lentil dhal

Calories per serving **466**
Serves **4**
Preparation time **15 minutes**
Cooking time **45 minutes**

2 teaspoons **ground cumin**
1 teaspoon **ground coriander**
½ teaspoon **cayenne pepper**
¼ teaspoon **ground turmeric**
500 g (1 lb) skinless, boneless
   chicken thighs, cut into
   large pieces
2 tablespoons **groundnut oil**
1 **onion**, sliced
2 garlic **cloves**, crushed
25 g (1 oz) **fresh root ginger**,
   peeled and finely chopped
750 ml (1¼ pints) **water**
300 g (10 oz) **red lentils**,
   rinsed
200 g (7 oz) **okra**
small handful of **fresh
   coriander** leaves, chopped
salt
lime wedges, to garnish

Mix the cumin, coriander, cayenne and turmeric and toss with the chicken pieces.

Heat the oil in a large saucepan. Fry the chicken pieces in batches until deep golden, transferring each batch to a plate. Add the onion to the pan and fry for 5 minutes until golden. Stir in the garlic and ginger and cook for a further 1 minute.

Return the chicken to the pan and add the measured water. Bring to the boil, reduce the heat and simmer very gently, covered, for 20 minutes until the chicken is cooked through. Add the lentils and cook for 5 minutes.

Stir in the okra, coriander and a little salt and cook for a further 5 minutes until the lentils are tender but not completely pulpy. Serve in shallow bowls with lime wedges.

For chicken, courgette & chilli dhal, follow the main recipe but replace the okra with 3 medium courgettes, thinly sliced. For a hotter flavour, add 1 thinly sliced medium-strength red chilli with the garlic and ginger.
Calories per serving 471

spicy lentils & chickpeas

Calories per serving **466**
Serves **4**
Preparation time **15 minutes**
Cooking time **about
    35 minutes**

1 tablespoon **groundnut oil**
1 **onion**, finely chopped
2 **garlic cloves**, thinly sliced
2 **celery sticks**, diced
1 **green pepper**, cored,
    deseeded and chopped
150 g (5 oz) **red lentils**, rinsed
2 teaspoons **garam masala**
    (see page 80)
1 teaspoon **cumin seeds**
½ teaspoon **hot chilli powder**
1 teaspoon **ground coriander**
2 tablespoons **tomato purée**
750 ml (1¼ pints) hot
    vegetable stock
400 g (13 oz) canned
    chickpeas, drained
salt and **pepper**
2 tablespoons chopped **fresh
    coriander**, to garnish
150 g (5 oz) boiled **brown rice**
    per person, to serve

Heat the oil in a heavy-based saucepan over a medium heat, add the onion, garlic, celery and green pepper and fry gently for 10–12 minutes or until softened and beginning to colour.

Stir in the lentils and spices and cook for 2–3 minutes, stirring frequently. Add the tomato purée, stock and chickpeas and bring to the boil. Reduce the heat, cover and simmer gently for about 20 minutes or until the lentils collapse. Season with salt and pepper to taste.

Ladle into bowls and sprinkle with the coriander. Serve immediately with boiled brown rice and cooling, spiced yogurt.

For cooling, spiced yogurt, to serve as an accompaniment, mix together 200 g (7 oz) fat-free natural yogurt, 2 tablespoons lemon juice and ½ teaspoon of garam masala in a small bowl. Fold in ½ a small, deseeded and grated cucumber, then season with salt and pepper to taste. Serve sprinkled with 1 tablespoon chopped coriander. **Calories per serving 33**

mango curry

Calories per serving **469**
Serves **4**
Preparation time **10 minutes**
Cooking time **8–10 minutes**

1 tablespoon **vegetable oil**
1 teaspoon **mustard seeds**
1 **onion**, halved and thinly
   sliced
15–20 **curry leaves, fresh**
   or **dried**
½ teaspoon **dried red chilli**
   flakes
1 teaspoon peeled and grated
   fresh root ginger
1 **green chilli**, deseeded and
   sliced
1 teaspoon **ground turmeric**
3 ripe **mangoes**, peeled,
   stoned and thinly sliced
400 ml (14 fl oz) **natural**
   yogurt, lightly beaten
salt
1 warm **chapati** per person,
   to serve

Heat the oil in a large saucepan until hot, add the mustard seeds, onion, curry leaves and chilli flakes and fry, stirring, for 4–5 minutes or until the onion is lightly browned.

Add the ginger and chilli and stir-fry for 1 minute, then add the turmeric and stir to mix well.

Remove the pan from the heat, add the mangoes and yogurt and stir continuously until well mixed. Season to taste with salt.

Return the pan to a low heat and heat through for 1 minute, stirring continuously. (Do not let it boil or the curry will curdle.) Serve immediately with 1 warm chapati per person.

For aubergine & pea curry, heat 1 tablespoon sunflower oil in a large frying pan until hot, then add 400 g (13 oz) peeled and cubed medium potatoes, 1 aubergine, cut into small chunks, 150 g (5 oz) frozen peas, 2 finely sliced onions, 2 crushed garlic cloves, 1 tablespoon ginger paste and 2 tablespoons medium curry powder. Stir-fry for 3–4 minutes or until the onion has softened and is turning golden, then pour in 600 ml (1 pint) chicken or vegetable stock and cook for 10–15 minutes or until the stock has reduced. Stir in 150 ml (¼ pint) reduced-fat crème fraîche and serve with ½ a large naan bread per person.
Calories per serving 473

green chicken curry

Calories per serving **469**
Serves **4**
Preparation time **15 minutes**
Cooking time **30–35 minutes**

1 tablespoon **sunflower oil**
3 tablespoons **Thai green curry paste** (see right)
2 **fresh green chillies**, finely chopped
750 g (1½ lb) boneless, skinless **chicken thighs**, cut into bite-sized pieces
400 ml (14 fl oz) can **coconut milk**
200 ml (7 fl oz) **chicken stock**
6 **lime leaves**
2 tablespoons **Thai fish sauce**
1 tablespoon **grated palm sugar**
200 g (7 oz) **pea aubergines**, or **standard aubergine**, diced
100 g (3½ oz) **green beans**, trimmed
50 g (2 oz) canned **bamboo shoots**, rinsed and drained
large handful of **Thai basil leaves**
large handful of **fresh coriander leaves**
4 tablespoons **lime juice**

Heat the oil in a large nonstick wok or saucepan and add the curry paste and chillies. Stir-fry for 2–3 minutes and then add the chicken. Stir and cook for 5–6 minutes or until the chicken is sealed and lightly browned.

Stir in the coconut milk, stock, lime leaves, fish sauce, palm sugar and pea aubergines. Simmer, uncovered for 10–15 minutes, stirring occasionally.

Add the green beans and bamboo shoots and continue to simmer for 6–8 minutes.

Remove from the heat and stir in the herbs and lime juice. Serve ladled into warmed bowls.

For homemade Thai green curry paste, blend the following ingredients to a smooth paste in a food processor: 4–6 long green chillies, chopped, 2 tablespoons chopped garlic, 2 tablespoons chopped lemon grass stalks, 4 shallots, finely chopped, 1 tablespoon finely chopped galangal or fresh root ginger, 2 teaspoons finely chopped lime leaves, 2 teaspoons ground coriander, 2 teaspoons ground cumin, 1 teaspoon white peppercorns, 2 teaspoons shrimp paste and 1 tablespoon groundnut oil. Store in an airtight container in the refrigerator for up to one month. **Calories per tablespoon 22**

squash, carrot & mango tagine

Calories per serving **474**
Serves **4**
Preparation time **15 minutes**
Cooking time **35–40 minutes**

2 tablespoons **olive oil**
1 large **onion**, cut into large
  chunks
3 **garlic cloves**, finely chopped
1 **butternut squash**, about
  875 g (1¾ lb) in total,
  peeled, deseeded and cubed
2 small **carrots**, peeled and
  cut into thick batons
½ × 2.5 cm (1 inch)
  cinnamon stick
½ teaspoon **turmeric**
¼ teaspoon **cayenne pepper**
  (optional)
½ teaspoon **ground cumin**
1 teaspoon **paprika**
pinch of **saffron threads**
1 tablespoon **tomato purée**
750 ml (1¼ pints) hot
  vegetable stock
1 **mango**, peeled, stoned
  and cut into 2.5 cm (1 inch)
  chunks
salt and **pepper**
2 tablespoons chopped **fresh**
  coriander, to garnish

Heat the oil in a large, heavy-based saucepan over a medium heat, add the onion and cook for 5 minutes or until beginning to soften. Add the garlic, squash, carrots and spices and fry gently for a further 5 minutes.

Stir in the tomato purée, then pour in the stock and season with salt and pepper to taste. Cover and simmer gently for 20–25 minutes or until the vegetables are tender. Stir in the mango and simmer gently for a further 5 minutes.

Ladle the tagine into serving bowls and sprinkle with the coriander and serve with steamed couscous.

For spicy squash & carrot soup, make the tagine as above, adding an extra 250 ml (8 fl oz) vegetable stock. Once the vegetables are tender, place in a food processor or blender and blend until smooth. Ladle into bowls and serve scattered with the chopped coriander.
Calories per serving 253

salmon curry with tomato salad

Calories per serving **477**
Serves **2**
Preparation time **10 minutes**
Cooking time **20 minutes**

1 teaspoon **vegetable oil**
1 **small onion**, sliced
1 **garlic clove**, chopped
1 teaspoon **tandoori spice mix**
1 **cinnamon stick**
150 g (5 oz) **cherry tomatoes**, halved
4 level tablespoons **reduced-fat crème fraîche**
grated rind and juice of ½ **lime**
175 g (6 oz) **skinless salmon fillet**, cut into chunks
1 tablespoon chopped **mint**
1 tablespoon chopped **fresh coriander**

Tomato & onion salad
150 g (5 oz) **vine-ripened tomatoes**, thinly sliced
1 **small red onion**, finely sliced
handful of **fresh coriander**, chopped
1 teaspoon **lemon juice**

Heat the oil in a small frying pan. Add the onion and garlic and fry for 2–3 minutes until softened. Stir in the spice mix and cinnamon stick and fry for a further minute. Add the tomatoes, crème fraîche, lime rind and juice and heat for a minute.

Put the salmon in an ovenproof dish. Spoon over the sauce, cover the dish tightly with foil and cook in a preheated oven, 200°C (400°F), Gas Mark 6, for 15–20 minutes or until the salmon is just cooked.

Meanwhile, make the salad by tossing together the tomatoes, onion and coriander. Dress with lemon juice.

Serve the salmon with the tomato and onion salad.

For paneer curry, prepare the sauce as above. Cut 150 g (5 oz) paneer into cubes and put the pieces in an ovenproof dish. Pour over the sauce, making sure the paneer cubes are evenly coated, cover with foil and cook as above. Serve with the tomato and onion salad.
Calories per serving 409

vegetable & rice noodle laksa

Calories per serving **479**
Serves **4**
Preparation time **20 minutes**
Cooking time **40 minutes**

1 tablespoon **groundnut oil**
2 tablespoons chopped **garlic**
1 tablespoon peeled and finely chopped **fresh root ginger**
2 **fresh red chillies**, sliced
2 **onions**, finely sliced
4 tablespoons **laksa curry paste**
300 ml (10 fl oz) **vegetable stock**
200 g (7 oz) **dried rice noodles**
400 ml (14 fl oz) can **reduced-fat coconut milk**
1 tablespoon **chilli bean sauce**
1 teaspoon **agave syrup**
50 g (2 oz) **bean sprouts**

To serve
4 **spring onions**, finely sliced
1 **fresh red chilli**, deseeded and thinly shredded
25 g (1 oz) finely chopped **fresh coriander leaves**
2 **eggs**, hard-boiled, peeled and halved
100 g (3½ oz) **roasted, skinless peanuts**, roughly chopped

Heat a wok or large frying pan over a high heat. Add the oil and, when it is starting to smoke, reduce the heat and add the garlic, ginger, chillies and onion. Stir-fry for 5 minutes. Add the curry paste and stock, reduce the heat to low, cover and simmer for 20 minutes.

Meanwhile, soak the rice noodles in a bowl of warm water for 20 minutes until tender, or according to the packet instructions. Drain well.

Add the coconut milk to the simmering liquid in the pan. Season with the chilli bean sauce and agave syrup, and add the bean sprouts. Continue simmering for a further 15 minutes.

Divide the noodles between 4 warmed serving bowls and ladle the coconut broth over the top. Serve immediately with the spring onions, chilli, coriander, eggs and peanuts in individual bowls, from which diners can help themselves.

For spicy vegetable & rice noodle stir-fry, heat 1 tablespoon groundnut oil in a large wok over a medium heat. Add 1 sliced onion, 3 thinly sliced garlic cloves, 1 teaspoon grated ginger and 2 sliced red chillies, and stir-fry for 2–3 minutes. Add a 400 g (13 oz) pack of prepared stir-fry vegetables and 300 g (10 oz) fresh rice noodles. Stir-fry for 3–4 minutes or until piping hot. Stir in 3 tablespoons light soy and 3 tablespoons sweet chilli sauce, toss to mix well and serve immediately. **Calories per serving 226**

asian lamb burgers

Calories per serving **480**
Serves **4**
Preparation time **20 minutes**
Cooking time **30 minutes**

2 **garlic cloves**, crushed
1 **lemon grass** stalk, finely
  chopped
25 g (1 oz) **fresh root ginger**,
  grated
large handful of **fresh
  coriander**, roughly chopped
1 **hot red chilli**, deseeded and
  thinly sliced
500 g (1 lb) **lean minced
  lamb**
2 tablespoons **oil**
1 **small cucumber**
1 bunch **spring onions**
200 g (7 oz) **pak choi**
3 tablespoons **light
  muscovado sugar**
finely grated rind of 2 **limes**,
  plus 4 tablespoons juice
2 tablespoons **fish sauce**
50 g (2 oz) **roasted peanuts**
salt

Blend the garlic, lemon grass, ginger, coriander, chilli and a little salt in a food processor to make a thick paste. Add the lamb and blend until mixed. Tip out on to the work surface and divide the mixture into 4 pieces. Roll each into a ball and flatten into a burger shape.

Heat the oil in a sturdy roasting pan and fry the burgers on both sides to sear. Transfer to a preheated oven, 200°C (400°F), Gas Mark 6, and cook, uncovered, for 25 minutes until the burgers are cooked through.

Meanwhile, peel the cucumber and cut in half lengthways. Scoop out the seeds with a teaspoon and discard. Cut the cucumber into thin, diagonal slices. Slice the spring onions diagonally. Roughly shred the pak choi; keep the white parts separate from the green.

Using a large metal spoon, drain off all but about 2 tablespoons fat from the roasting pan. Arrange all the vegetables except the green parts of the pak choi around the meat and toss them gently in the pan juices. Return to the oven, uncovered, for 5 minutes.

Mix together the sugar, lime rind and juice and fish sauce. Scatter the pak choi greens and peanuts into the roasting pan and drizzle with half the dressing.

Toss the salad ingredients together gently. Transfer the lamb and salad to serving plates and drizzle with the remaining dressing.

For chicken burgers, use minced chicken instead of the lamb. Replace the pak choi with shredded spring greens and peanuts with salted cashews. **Calories per serving 400**

crab & coconut chowder

Calories per serving **481**
Serves **4**
Preparation time **15 minutes**
Cooking time **50 minutes**

25 g (1 oz) **butter**
1 tablespoon **vegetable oil**
1 large **onion**, chopped
200 g (7 oz) **lean belly pork**,
  finely diced
2 **garlic cloves**, crushed
150 ml (¼ pint) **dry white wine**
200 g (7 oz) can **chopped
  tomatoes**
400 ml (14 fl oz) can **reduced-
  fat coconut milk**
1 teaspoon **medium curry
  paste**
350 g (12 oz) **waxy potatoes**,
  diced
300 g (10 oz) **white** and
  brown crabmeat
3 tablespoons **double cream**
salt and **pepper**

Melt the butter with the oil in a large saucepan and gently fry the onion and pork, stirring, for about 10 minutes until lightly browned. Stir in the garlic and fry for 1 minute. Lift the pork out with a slotted spoon on to a plate.

Add the wine to the pan, bring to the boil and boil for about 5 minutes, until slightly reduced.

Return the pork to the pan, add the tomatoes, coconut milk, curry paste and potatoes and heat until simmering. Reduce the heat to its lowest setting, cover and cook for 30 minutes.

Stir in the crabmeat and cream, heat through thoroughly, and season to taste with salt and pepper. Serve hot with crusty bread, if liked.

For smoked haddock & sweetcorn chowder, melt 25 g (1 oz) butter in a large saucepan and gently fry 1 chopped onion and 1 chopped celery stick. Stir in 2 teaspoons crushed coriander seeds, ¼ teaspoon ground turmeric, 600 ml (1 pint) milk and 450 ml (¾ pint) fish or chicken stock. Bring just to the boil, then reduce the heat to its lowest setting. Stir in 500 g (1 lb) diced waxy potatoes and 625 g (1¼ lb) diced skinless smoked haddock fillet. Cover and cook gently for 10 minutes, then stir in 200 g (7 oz) sweetcorn and cook for a further 10 minutes. Season to taste with pepper and serve. **Calories per serving 428**

lime, ginger & coriander chicken

Calories per serving **482**
Serves **4**
Preparation time
5–10 minutes
Cooking time **50 minutes**

3 **limes**
1 cm (½ inch) cube **fresh root
   ginger**, peeled and finely
   grated
4 tablespoons finely chopped
   fresh coriander, plus extra
   leaves to serve
2 teaspoons **vegetable oil**
4 **chicken legs**
150 g (5 oz) steamed **rice** per
   person, to serve
salt

Finely grate the rind of 2 of the limes and halve these limes. Mix the rind with the ginger and coriander in a non-metallic bowl and stir in 1 teaspoon of the oil to make a rough paste.

Carefully lift the skin from the chicken legs and push under the ginger paste. Pull the skin back into place, then cut 3–4 slashes in the thickest parts of the legs and brush with the remaining oil.

Put the legs in a roasting tin, flesh-side down, with the halved limes and cook in a preheated oven, 220°C (425°F), Gas Mark 7, for 45–50 minutes, basting occasionally. The legs are cooked when the meat comes away from the bone and the juices run clear.

Spoon the rice into small bowls to mould, then turn it on to serving plates. Add the chicken legs, squeeze over the roasted lime and scatter with coriander leaves. Serve immediately with the remaining lime, cut into wedges, and rice.

For Mediterranean chicken, replace the ginger paste with a red pesto made by blending 6 sun-dried tomatoes, 1 tablespoon pine nuts, ½ clove chopped garlic, 1 tablespoon chopped basil, 1 teaspoon grated lemon rind, 1 tablespoon lemon juice, 2 tablespoons olive oil and 1 tablespoon grated Parmesan cheese. **Calories per serving 499**

caribbean lamb stoba

Calories per serving **483**
Serves **4**
Preparation time **25 minutes**
Cooking time 1¾ **hours**

1 tablespoon **groundnut oil**
750 g (1½ lb) **lean lamb,**
   cubed
2 **onions,** finely chopped
2 teaspoons finely grated
   fresh root ginger
1 **scotch bonnet chilli,** thinly
   sliced
1 **red pepper,** cored,
   deseeded and roughly
   chopped
2 teaspoons **ground allspice**
3 teaspoons **ground cumin**
1 **cinnamon stick**
pinch of grated **nutmeg**
400 g (13 oz) can **chopped
   tomatoes**
300 g (10 oz) **cherry tomatoes**
finely grated rind and juice of
   2 **limes**
65 g (2½ oz) **soft brown sugar**
200 g (7 oz) fresh or frozen
   peas
salt and **pepper**

Heat half the oil in a large saucepan. Brown the lamb in batches for 3–4 minutes. Remove with a slotted spoon and set aside.

Heat the remaining oil in the saucepan and add the onion, ginger, chilli, red pepper and spices. Stir-fry for 3–4 minutes then add the lamb with the canned and cherry tomatoes, lime rind and juice, and sugar. Season and bring to the boil. Reduce the heat, cover tightly and simmer gently for 1½ hours or until the lamb is tender.

Stir in the peas 5 minutes before serving on warmed plates with rice.

mustard, mango & yogurt curry

Calories per serving **491**
Serves **4**
Preparation time **20 minutes**
Cooking time **about 20
  minutes**

300 g (10 oz) **fresh coconut,**
  grated
3–4 **fresh green chillies,**
  roughly chopped
1 tablespoon **cumin seeds**
500 ml (17 fl oz) **water**
3 firm, ripe **mangoes,** peeled,
  stoned and cubed
1 teaspoon **ground turmeric**
1 teaspoon **chilli powder**
300 ml (½ pint) **fat-free
  natural yogurt,** lightly
  whisked
1 tablespoon **groundnut oil**
2 teaspoons **black mustard
  seeds**
3–4 **hot dried red chillies**
10–12 **curry leaves**

Place the coconut, green chillies and cumin seeds in a
food processor with half the measured water and blend
to a fine paste.

Place the mangoes in a heavy saucepan with the
turmeric, chilli powder and the remaining measured
water. Bring to the boil, add the coconut paste and stir
to mix well. Cover and simmer over a medium heat for
10–12 minutes, stirring occasionally, until the mixture
becomes fairly thick.

Add the yogurt and heat gently, stirring, until just
warmed through. Do not let the mixture come to the boil
or it will curdle. Remove from the heat and keep warm.

Heat the oil in a small pan over a medium-high heat.
Add the mustard seeds and as soon as they begin to
'pop' (after a few seconds), add the dried chillies and
curry leaves. Stir-fry for a few seconds until the chillies
darken. Stir the spice mixture into the mango curry and
serve immediately.

For spicy mango & mint salad, peel, stone and cube
4 ripe mangoes. Place in a serving dish with ½ thinly
sliced red onion, 12 halved cherry tomatoes and a large
handful of mint leaves. Make a dressing by whisking
200 ml (7 fl oz) fat-free natural yogurt with the juice of
1 lime, 1 teaspoon agave syrup and 1 finely diced red
chilli. Season, drizzle over the salad, toss to mix well and
serve. **Calories per serving 204**

mixed bean kedgeree

Calories per serving **497**
Serves **4**
Preparation time **10 minutes**
Cooking time **15–20 minutes**

1 tablespoon **olive oil**
1 **onion**, chopped
2 tablespoons **mild curry powder**
225 g (7 ½ oz) **long-grain rice**
750 ml (1 ¼ pints) **vegetable stock**
4 **eggs**
2 × 400 g (13 oz) cans **mixed beans**, drained and rinsed
150 ml (¼ pint) **fat-free fromage frais**
salt and **pepper**
2 **tomatoes**, finely chopped, to garnish
flat leaf parsley, to garnish

Heat the oil in a saucepan, add the onion and cook until soft. Stir in the curry powder and rice. Add the stock and season to taste with salt and pepper. Bring to the boil, then reduce the heat, cover and simmer, stirring occasionally, for 10–15 minutes until all the stock has been absorbed and the rice is tender.

Meanwhile, put the eggs in a saucepan of cold water and bring to the boil. Cook for 10 minutes, then plunge into cold water to cool. Shell the eggs, then cut them into wedges.

Stir through the beans and fromage frais and cook briefly over a low heat to heat through. Serve garnished with the eggs, tomatoes and parsley.

turkish lamb & spinach curry

Calories per serving **497**
Serves **4**
Preparation time **20 minutes**
Cooking time **2 hours**

4 tablespoons **sunflower oil**
600 g (1 lb 4 oz) **boneless
  shoulder of lamb**, cut into
  bite-sized pieces
1 **onion**, finely chopped
3 **garlic cloves**, crushed
1 teaspoon **ground ginger**
2 teaspoons **ground turmeric**
large pinch of **grated nutmeg**
4 tablespoons **sultanas**
1 teaspoon **ground cinnamon**
1 teaspoon **paprika**
400 g (13 oz) canned
  chopped tomatoes
300 ml (½ pint) **lamb stock**
400 g (13 oz) **baby leaf
  spinach**
salt and **pepper**

Heat half the oil in a large, heavy-based saucepan and brown the lamb, in batches, for 3–4 minutes. Remove with a slotted spoon and set aside.

Heat the remaining oil in the pan and add the onion, garlic, ginger, turmeric, nutmeg, sultanas, cinnamon and paprika. Stir-fry for 1–2 minutes and then add the lamb. Stir-fry for a further 2–3 minutes and then add the tomatoes and stock. Season well and bring to the boil.

Reduce the heat, cover tightly and simmer very gently (using a heat diffuser if possible) for 1½ hours.

Add the spinach in batches until it is all wilted, cover and cook for a further 10–12 minutes, stirring occasionally. Remove from the heat and serve drizzled with whisked yogurt, if liked.

For Turkish lamb & aubergine curry, use a large aubergine instead of the spinach. Cut the aubergine into bite-sized chunks and fry it in oil until light golden brown, along with the lamb. You may need to add a little more oil to fry the aubergine. **Calories per serving 475**

coconut lamb curry

Calories per serving **497**
Serves **4**
Preparation time **15 minutes**
Cooking time **about 2 hours**

2 tablespoons **sunflower oil**
1 **onion**, thinly sliced
2 teaspoons grated **fresh root ginger**
2 teaspoons **crushed garlic**
1 teaspoon **ground cinnamon**
20 **curry leaves**
2 tablespoons **mild curry powder**
1 tablespoon **ground coriander**
1 teaspoon **ground turmeric**
1 teaspoon **chilli powder**
625 g (1¼ lb) **boneless lamb**, cut into chunks
400 ml (14 fl oz) can **coconut milk**
200 ml (7 fl oz) **vegetable stock**
100 g (3½ oz) **fresh coconut**, grated
6 tablespoons chopped **fresh coriander**
salt and **pepper**

Heat the oil in a large, heavy-based saucepan.

Add the onion and stir-fry over a medium heat for 4–5 minutes. Stir in the ginger, garlic, cinnamon, curry leaves, curry powder, ground coriander, turmeric and chilli powder. Stir-fry for 2–3 minutes and then add the lamb.

Stir-fry for 2–3 minutes and then stir in the coconut milk and stock. Bring to the boil, season well and cover tightly. Cook over a very low heat (using a heat diffuser if possible), stirring occasionally, for 1½–2 hours or until the lamb is tender. Remove from the heat and sprinkle over the grated coconut and chopped fresh coriander before serving.

For coconut chicken curry, use 750 g (1½ lb) skinless chicken thighs on the bone, instead of the lamb, and reduce the cooking time to 1–1½ hours. After 1 hour add ½ small cauliflower, cut into florets, and 250 g (8 oz) carrots, peeled, halved lengthways and sliced. Sprinkle in 50 g (2 oz) sultanas or raisins, if liked.
Calories per serving 495

thai green pork curry

Calories per serving **498**
Serves **4**
Preparation time **10 minutes**
Cooking time **20 minutes**

2 tablespoons **olive oil**
4 boneless **pork steaks**, cut
  into bite-sized pieces
2 tablespoons **Thai green
  curry paste** (see page 208)
400 ml (14 fl oz) can **coconut
  milk**
100 g (3½ oz) **green beans**
200 g (7 oz) can **water
  chestnuts**, drained, rinsed
  and cut in half
juice of 1 **lime**, or to taste
1 handful of **fresh coriander
  leaves**

Heat the oil in a large saucepan, add the pork and cook, stirring, for 3–4 minutes until browned all over. Add the curry paste and cook, stirring, for 1 minute until fragrant.

Add the coconut milk, stir and reduce the heat to a gentle simmer. Cook for 10 minutes, then add the beans and water chestnuts. Cook for a further 3 minutes.

Remove from the heat, add lime juice to taste and stir through the coriander. Serve immediately with boiled rice.

For Thai red pork curry, replace the Thai green curry paste with Thai red curry paste. To prepare your own Thai red curry paste, put 10 large red chillies, 2 teaspoons coriander seeds, 5 cm (2 inch) piece of fresh root ginger, peeled and finely chopped, 1 finely chopped lemon grass stalk, 4 halved garlic cloves, 1 roughly chopped shallot, 1 teaspoon lime juice and 2 tablespoons groundnut oil in a food processor or blender and process to a thick paste. Alternatively, pound the ingredients together using a pestle and mortar. Transfer the paste to an airtight container; it can be stored in the refrigerator for up to 3 weeks.
Calories per serving 498

kheema mutter

Calories per serving **499**
Serves **4**
Preparation time **20 minutes**
Cooking time **1½–2 hours**

2 tablespoons **sunflower oil**
1 **large onion**, finely chopped
3 **garlic cloves**, crushed
1 teaspoon **finely grated
   fresh root ginger**
3–4 **fresh green chillies**,
   deseeded and finely sliced
1 tablespoon **cumin seeds**
3 tablespoons **hot curry paste**
750 g (1½ lb) **minced beef**
400 g (13 oz) canned
   chopped tomatoes
1 teaspoon **sugar**
4 tablespoons **tomato purée**
4 tablespoons **coconut cream**
250 g (8 oz) **fresh** or **frozen
   peas**
salt and **pepper**
large handful of chopped **fresh
   coriander**, to garnish

Heat the oil in a large, heavy-based saucepan and add the onion. Cook over a low heat for 15–20 minutes, until softened and just turning light golden-brown.

Add the garlic, ginger, chilli, cumin seeds and curry paste and stir-fry over a high heat for 1–2 minutes.

Add the minced beef and stir-fry for 3–4 minutes. Stir in the tomatoes, sugar and tomato purée and bring to the boil. Season well, cover and reduce the heat to low. Cook for 1–1½ hours until the mince is tender.

Pour in the coconut cream and add the peas 10 minutes before the end of cooking time. Garnish with the chopped coriander and serve lime slices and red chillies as well as rice or a naan, if liked.

index

acknowledgements

Commissioning Editor: Eleanor Maxfield
Design: Jeremy Tilston & Jaz Bahra
Assistant Production Manager: Caroline Alberti

Photography copyright © Octopus Publishing Group/
Frank Adam 33. Stephen Conroy 1, 2–3, 6–7, 14, 15,
18–19, 30, 49, 53, 55, 61–62, 67, 69, 71, 91, 93, 103,
107, 108-109, 113, 119, 127, 133, 137, 139, 145, 147,
151, 153, 155, 161, 169, 173, 175, 177, 179, 183, 185,
191, 195, 197, 209, 213, 221, 223, 227, 229, 231,
233, 235. Will Heap 4–5, 8, 10, 11, 16, 25, 35, 37, 39,
43, 45, 47, 57, 59, 65, 73, 75, 79, 81, 85, 97, 105, 111,
115, 121, 123, 125, 131, 135, 143, 149, 171, 181,
187, 189, 201, 207, 215, 225. William Lingwood 99.
Neil Mersh 89. David Munns 117, 157, 193.
Lis Parsons 13, 137, 141, 165, 166-167, 203, 217.
Gareth Sambidge 27, 41. William Shaw 83, 101, 205,
211, 219. William Reavell 23, 29, 31, 51, 77, 129, 159,
163. Ian Wallace 87, 95, 199.